camus

camus

PORTRAIT OF A MORALIST

Stephen Eric Bronner

University of Minnesota Press Minneapolis — London

Published by the University of Minnesota Press
111 Third Avenue South, Suite 290
Minneapolis, MN 55401-2520
http://www.upress.umn.edu

Printed in the United States of America on acid-free paper

Library of Congress Cataloging-in-Publication Data

Bronner, Stephen Eric, 1949–
    Camus : portrait of a moralist / Stephen Eric Bronner.
        p.   cm.
    Includes bibliographical references and index.
    ISBN 0-8166-3283-9 (hardcover). — ISBN 0-8166-3284-7
(pbk.)
    1. Camus, Albert, 1913–1960—Ethics.   I. Title.
PQ2605.A3734Z6256   1999
848'.91409— dc21   98-51470

The University of Minnesota is an equal-opportunity educator
and employer.

11 10 09 08 07 06 05 04 03 02 01 00 99
10 9 8 7 6 5 4 3 2 1

For two old friends who remain in my thoughts:

Peter Pappas
and
Maurice Trauring

contents

preface

Every great writer touches the young, and Albert Camus was no exception. He spoke to his generation, which came of age in the 1940s and 1950s. But he was also the most popular writer among the students of the 1960s. His works still exert a remarkable influence. Part of the reason, perhaps, derives from his paradoxical image. Camus was an artist who dealt with the perennial concerns of philosophy. He hated existentialism, but popularized many of its basic ideas. He was a man of the Mediterranean who lived in Europe. He was a modernist with a classical style. He was a member of the antifascist resistance, but also a pacifist. He was a partisan and a private person. He was an intellectual and also a celebrity with a trenchcoat and a cigarette who liked to style himself after Humphrey Bogart.

Above all, Camus was the great *moraliste* of twentieth-century French letters. His blend of idealism and skepticism, integrity and egoism, public commitment and private passion, belief in rebellion and recognition of limits, made him popular among advocates of the most diverse forms of political philosophy. Postmodernists and conservatives alike now arbitrarily employ Camus in order to justify their agendas; it doesn't seem to matter that his thinking was profoundly "essentialist" or that he was an engaged critic of the capitalist status quo. Given the diverse elements of his thought, his refusal to identify himself with any given school, Camus has often been employed for the purpose of legitimating even those positions with which he profoundly disagreed. In any event, this study is content to offer a revamped portrait of Camus, which nevertheless remains true to his explicit socialist and liberal commitments. It takes the overarching traditions influencing him into account, refuses to divorce his art from his politics, and seeks to deal judiciously with the relevance of his ideas for the present.

The library stacks overflow with books on his career. And precious little factual information about Camus is missing. There are two huge and splendidly researched biographies, but they share an inability to distinguish the essential from the inessential, and they privilege the personal over the political and the philosophical.[1] These works are complemented by a host of introductory studies, scholarly anthologies, and esoteric monographs. Some are strong on the politics and weak on the philosophy;[2] others are better on the philosophy than the politics.[3] Most sec-

1. Herbert Lottman, *Albert Camus: A Biography* (New York, 1979); Olivier Todd, *Albert Camus: une vie* (Paris, 1996). The English translation of the latter work, *Albert Camus: A Life,* trans. Benjamin Ivry (New York, 1997), has been edited to half its former length, and the interpretive weaknesses only become more glaring in this truncated version of the original.

2. Jeanyves Guérin, *Camus: portrait de l'artiste en citoyen* (Paris, 1993).

3. David Sprintzen, *Camus: A Critical Examination* (Philadelphia, 1988).

ondary works are manifestly uncritical;[4] others are decidedly tendentious.[5] Few offer a balanced philosophical, artistic, and political treatment of his work. Even fewer combine an overview of the grand themes with more sophisticated internal and historical interpretations over which specialists can argue.

This volume is an attempt to fill the gap. It also seeks to provide new interpretations of his major texts, his politics, and his worldview. It takes seriously Camus's unique use of the classical heritage. It doesn't accept at face value his staunch rejection of existentialism and it emphasizes the influence of his dissertation on his later thought; it also presents his secular philosophy as informed by the Christianity it ostensibly wishes to oppose. My study reinterprets *The Stranger* as a modern variant of the educational novel; it offers a new view on *The Myth of Sisyphus;* it deals with the implications of *The Plague* as a realistic parable; it treats *The Fall* as a meditation on authenticity; and it offers a new interpretation of his posthumously published *The First Man.* The present work rethinks the philosophic assumptions of major plays like *Caligula* and *The Just,* the idea that resistance against oppression is somehow connected with a recognition of the absurd, and it confronts the ambiguous subjectivism underpinning less influential works like *Exile and the Kingdom.* It offers a new look at the famous conflict between Camus and Jean-

4. Germaine Brée, *Camus* (New Brunswick, 1972); Emmett Parker, *The Artist in the Arena* (Madison, 1965); Roger Quilliot, *The Sea and Prisons: A Commentary on the Life and Thought of Albert Camus,* trans. Emmett Parker (Tuscaloosa, 1970).

5. Patrick McCarthy, *Camus: A Critical Study of His Life and Works* (London, 1982); Conor Cruise O'Brien, *Albert Camus of Europe and Africa* (New York, 1970).

Preface

Paul Sartre; it provides a new take on Camus and the Algerian conflict; and it gives a new interpretation of his more general ideas concerning resistance and revolution, which receive explicit expression in *The Rebel,* in the light of a new "postcommunist" environment. This study also rejects the often artificial divorce made by critics between the art and the politics of Camus. Indeed, for better or worse, it understands his writings as a single exercise in symbolic action.

The present volume is a work of intellectual history with a political intent. It charts the career of Camus through his works and interventions, places them in a determinate context, and provides new insights for all of them. But it refuses to choose between a sociological and a formal analysis. It sees the need for an interplay between them in order to illuminate the unacknowledged material sources of the ideas and their salience for our time. Such an approach makes clear how, with Camus, the ethical interest always permeates the way in which it is expressed. The form is inextricably interwoven with the content, and his work illustrates an obsession with the *craft* of writing. Camus trespasses the boundaries between art, politics, and philosophy, even while leaving them intact. He provides his readers, in the most basic sense, with a *literature of moral deliberation.*

The phrase does not need "deep" psychological or philosophical definition. Camus contests the popular relativism of our time. His nobility of sentiment and his willingness to engage in the reconstruction of freedom offer a welcome antidote to the dissolute cynicism and the preoccupation with deconstructing ideas so common among contemporary intellectuals.

I first read Camus as a teenager. I remember applauding

his contempt for totalitarianism and his humanism, his strange mixture of pessimism and optimism, and his ability to engage himself in the political world without forgetting about the desire for personal happiness and sensuous experience. But, ultimately, something else made him special. An aura of decency and charity surrounded him: there was something unique about his sense of personal responsibility, his lucidity, his tolerance, and his honesty. The best homage for such a man is less an exhibition of reverence than a critical encounter in which the salience of his work is not simply taken for granted. That is what this book seeks to provide.

1 — early days

*The men of my race arrive on wingless,
eyeless ships.*

       —André Malraux

YOUTH

Albert Camus was born on November 7, 1913, in Algeria. He grew to maturity in this French colony, and the experience enabled him later to become a man of two continents. Interestingly enough, whatever the political problems, he rarely felt the existential tension of living in two cultures. Perhaps that is because Algeria, unlike other colonies, was always considered part of France, especially by its white settlers, or *pieds-noirs*. They had come in droves following the Franco-Prussian War of 1871 when 250,000 acres in the North African colony were given to citizens opting for French nationality from the hotly contested province of Alsace-Lorraine.[1] Camus would later describe their troubles and difficulties in the new land. His father, Lucien Auguste Camus, was born in 1885 and placed in an orphanage as a young child by his four older brothers and sisters. He taught himself to read and write and, after running away from the orphanage, became an apprentice in a vineyard in the Algerian town of Cheraga, where he met his future wife, Catherine Sintes.

1. Lottman, *Albert Camus,* 8.

1

The young couple was soon separated. Lucien Auguste was drafted in 1906 and spent the next two years performing military service in Casablanca while Catherine, three years his senior, moved with her family to the Belcourt section of Algiers. Upon his discharge from the military in 1908, refusing to reconcile with the siblings who had exiled him to the orphanage, Lucien Auguste joined her. They married in 1909. A year later, Lucien Camus was born. A job with a wine company led the father to settle his family near the village of Mondavi. There they remained after Catherine Sintes gave birth to Albert and learned of her husband's death, shortly after he was called up, in the Battle of the Marne.

Albert Camus had few memories of his father; he was one year old when his father died. He would always remain close to his brother Lucien, and his mother would figure prominently in his first collection of essays and later in his anguished reflections on the Algerian War. She was of Spanish origin and illiterate. One of nine children, whose ancestors had migrated to Algeria in 1850, she was deaf and suffered from a speech impediment caused by an untreated illness during her childhood. Following the death of her husband, without any resources, she moved back to the home of her deeply religious mother in the proletarian neighborhood of Belcourt, where they and the two children shared a three-room apartment with her two older brothers, Joseph and Étienne. The former left the family's home in 1920; the latter was born mute and, after an operation at the age of thirteen, could speak only with difficulty. He worked at a cooperage and Catherine cleaned houses. Both were subservient to their domineering mother, who was known to discipline her grandchildren with a whip. It was, in short, a bleak existence. The situation is described by Albert Camus as follows:

There were five of them living together: the grandmother, her younger son, her elder daughter, and the
daughter's two children. The son was almost dumb;
the daughter, an invalid, could only think with difficulty; and of the two children, one was already working for an insurance company while the other was
continuing his studies. At seventy, the grandmother
still dominated all these people . . . With enormous
clear, cold eyes, she had a regal posture she relin-
quished only with increasing age, but which she still
sometimes tried to recover when she went out.[2]

The poverty in which Camus grew to maturity was
both material and emotional. There were no books in his
home. His grandmother and mother never joked or chat-
ted; they were fatalistic, pessimistic, and stoic. The uncle
didn't help matters. It was a hard existence compounded
by economic want. "A certain number of years lived without money," Camus could write, "are enough to create a
whole sensibility."[3]

But Camus never really complained about his impoverished childhood. Moments of happiness were savored.
He was eloquent in stating how, despite all the poverty,
Algeria could not compare with the misery of the cold
and gray slums of Europe. His early experiences gave him
the ability later to speak with people from all classes. His
childhood taught him a singular understanding of misery,

2. Albert Camus, "The Wrong Side and the Right Side," in *Lyrical and
Critical Essays*, ed. Philip Thody, trans. Ellen Conroy Kennedy (New
York, 1968), 27. Subsequent page references to this work appear paren-
thetically in the text.

3. Albert Camus, *Notebooks*, 2 vols., trans. Justin O'Brien (New York,
1991), 1: 3.

which made his empathy with the disempowered genuine. The racially mixed character of Belcourt with its Jews, Europeans, and Muslims,[4] whether Camus understated the degree of tension between them or not, surely provided him with his cosmopolitan outlook. It also helped create in Camus a hatred of intolerance, especially the arrogance and racism of the French in regard to the Arabs.

His childhood, undeniably, left scars. A hint of the reserve and sobriety, the reflexive distance, would remain. He would always feel the need to prove himself, with women as well as with work, and he often indulged in acting the tough. Jean Grenier, his teacher and friend, noted these qualities in the young man and wrote that "his adolescence was accompanied by a general contempt for the entire world and a will to personal domination."[5] A desire to succeed and a dislike of the price such success exacts, a sense of superiority and a feeling of inferiority, often go together. The tension would never leave him.

The relations between Camus and his teachers partially compensated for the emotional emptiness he experienced at home. As a child, from 1918 to 1923, he attended public school. There he met Louis Germain, who was a "second father to Albert—or perhaps the first,"[6] and to whom he would dedicate his acceptance speech for the Nobel Prize in 1957. The teacher recognized the talent of the young Camus and took a liking to him. Germain helped Camus, a model student, win a high school scholarship in 1924 to the *Grand lycées*. He apparently advocated liberal principles,[7] like so many of his profession, and Germain un-

4. Brée, *Camus*, 12.
5. Jean Grenier, *Albert Camus: Souvenirs* (Paris, 1968), 13.
6. Todd, *Albert Camus*, 30.
7. McCarthy, *Camus*, 15.

doubtedly helped instill respect for democratic values in his prize pupil. On receiving the Nobel Prize, Camus wrote a letter to Germain, which beautifully expressed his feelings:

> When I heard the news, my first thought, after my mother, was of you. Without you, without the affectionate hand you extended to the small poor child that I was, without your teaching, and your example, none of all this would have happened. But at least it gives me an opportunity to tell you what you have been and still are for me, and to assure you that your efforts, your work, and the generous heart you put into it still live in one of your little schoolboys who, despite the years, has never stopped being your grateful pupil.[8]

For all his interest in school, however, the young man was also preoccupied with soccer and, as he grew older, hanging around Algiers with his friends from the neighborhood. "Innocence" was the word he used to describe his youth. But things changed around 1930 when Camus learned he was suffering from tuberculosis; it provided what André Gide might have called a "rendez-vous with sensations." He spent one year recuperating with the family of his uncle Gustave Acault, an autodidact and a remarkable personality who worked as a butcher, and then another year studying for his baccalaureate, which he received in 1932. Acault had befriended the young man earlier and helped introduce him to modern literature.

In 1930 Camus also met the man who would exert the

---

8. From "Two Letters," appended to Albert Camus, *The First Man*, trans. David Hapgood (New York, 1995), 321.

most profound influence on his career: Jean Grenier.[9] The author of *Islands* (1933) and *Mediterranean Inspirations* (1941), a passionate democrat and a committed teacher, Grenier had left France for Algeria in order to experience a new culture. As his high school philosophy teacher, Grenier opened Camus to the world of ideas, particularly the thinking of Bergson and Nietzsche. More than that, he put his own stamp on his student. A friend of André Malraux and Gide, whom he met while working briefly for the publishing house Gallimard and writing for the prestigious *Nouvelle Revue Française,* Grenier viewed European civilization as decadent. He opposed it to the earlier vitality of Greek literature and philosophy beginning with Plato. He provided his student with an exhilarating insight into the "pagan" heritage of classical Greece and saw a source of renewal in what Camus would later call the "Mediterranean temperament."

Grenier also had an impact on the art of Camus. *Islands,* which was composed of experiential fragments, inspired the style of two essay collections by Grenier's prodigy. Its "pagan" concern with sensuality and natural beauty, which contrasts so starkly with the rationalizing forces of "civilization," would influence Camus's choice of themes as surely as the emphasis placed by Grenier on loneliness and death. People are described by Grenier as

9. "Grenier's relationship with Camus is often misunderstood . . . If he had cared more for Grenier, he might have publicized his gratitude less, for it mortified Grenier, who saw himself robbed of his own originality and reduced to an appendage of Camus. The post-war Camus-Grenier relationship was full of concealed hypocrisies which lay beyond the master-pupil effusions and by the end Camus was thoroughly sick of him. Meanwhile Grenier fought back by telling everyone that he had done little for Camus, no more than for other students." McCarthy, *Camus,* 32 ff. passim.

stranded on deserted islands, lonely, bereft of hope, and without systematic philosophical answers to the deepest questions regarding the meaning of life or the character of happiness. As a young man, Camus could say of *Islands* and his teacher:

> Have read Grenier's book. He puts his whole self in it and I feel the admiration and the love he inspires in me grow. Of him it can be said that he assumes the greatest possible humanity precisely by trying to keep his distance from it. The unity of his book is the constant presence of death. This makes it clear why the very sight of G., though not changing anything about the way I am, makes me graver, more deeply concerned about the gravity of life.[10]

The writings of Grenier, like the future works of his pupil, blend a simplicity of form with the illumination of personal experience. A preoccupation with death also bound the two men. Grenier saw death as rounding out human existence and creating an "amputated being" or a life always cut short. His notion must have deeply affected Camus when the young man learned of his tuberculosis and, with bitter irony, became forced to confront his mortality in a new way.[11] Indeed, when combined with the Catholicism inherited from his deeply religious mother, this looming presence of death helps explain the obsession with God and theological questions that would remain with Camus throughout his life.[12]

Issues of personal responsibility, fate, and life's meaning

10. Albert Camus, *Youthful Writings,* trans. Ellen Conroy Kennedy (New York, 1976), 178.

11. Lottman, *Albert Camus,* 46.

12. Abdallah Naaman, *La Mort et Camus* (Paris, 1980), 49 ff. passim.

also surely assumed added importance following Camus's disastrous marriage to Simone Hié in 1934.[13] A year younger than Camus, by all accounts she was a talented actress and extraordinarily beautiful. A bohemian and a nonconformist, the daughter of a noted radical doctor, she became addicted to morphine around the age of fourteen. When she met Camus in 1932, Simone was engaged to marry one of his best friends, a leader of the Federation of Young Socialists in Algeria named Max-Pol Fouchet. She soon transferred her affections, and the friendship between the young men ended. The Acaults, with whom Camus was still living, were appalled. They disapproved of Simone and thought their nephew's intention to marry her was a big mistake. Arguments between Gustave and Albert grew more frequent and more heated. Camus finally left and moved in briefly with his brother Lucien. With financial support from his future mother-in-law and the wages he earned tutoring high school students, Camus entered the University of Algiers in 1933.

A year later he and Simone were married. Things went well at first; they traveled and even attended classes together. With relative speed, however, their relationship became dominated by unsuccessful attempts to overcome her addiction, coupled with her stratagems to maintain her habit, including sleeping with her doctors for drugs. Camus was mortified. Initially, he believed he could cure his wife. But he was wrong. Her condition deteriorated. She became more erratic. She often embarrassed him in public and slept with his friends. They drifted apart, but didn't divorce until 1940, when Camus decided to marry

13. Todd, *Albert Camus,* 60 ff.

Francine Faure, a pretty if physically delicate mathematician from a provincial middle-class family in Oran. His affection for Simone remained, and during the ensuing years he complied whenever she requested money for her addiction.[14] She died in 1970, nearly a decade after her ex-husband.

During the difficult time of his involvement and break-up with Simone Hié, Camus also met two young students, Jeanne-Paul Sicard and Marguerite Dobrenn, with whom he would remain close friends until the end of his life. Both were interested in the theater and the arts; both were bohemians and members of the Communist Party in their youth; both moved toward General Charles de Gaulle during the Resistance; both became important political functionaries in the postwar era; and both, for a few years beginning in 1935, shared a residence with Camus high above Algiers. It would become his refuge: the House at the Edge of the World.

Camus paid a high price for his relationship with Simone Hié. He alienated friends and family. But, strangely enough, he was able to divorce his private from his public existence. Camus decided to enter the University of Algiers in 1933, and, soon enough, Grenier joined the faculty. Their relationship continued as Camus wrote the thesis for which he would receive his diploma in philosophy in 1936. It is a difficult text and rarely analyzed, but *Christian Metaphysics and Neoplatonism* provides a deep insight into the hotly contested issue of Camus's relation to religion.[15]

14. Ibid., 113 ff.

15. Camus's dissertation is reprinted, with a fine scholarly commentary by Joseph McBride, as *Albert Camus: Philosopher and Litterateur* (New York, 1992), 77 ff.

Early Days

It is fashionable now to ignore the influence of Christianity on Camus, but his dissertation gives excellent insight into this often-neglected connection. The study was primarily concerned with the way in which Christianity gradually embraced Hellenism, the ideals of ancient Greece. This is a matter of importance insofar as rational knowledge and worldly experience, which constitute basic elements of the Hellenic legacy, seemingly stand in stark opposition to the emphasis Christian religion places on revelatory faith and the inner life. These conflicting tendencies would manifest themselves in all of Camus's later writings. It is also noteworthy that the two most prominent philosophers discussed in his thesis, Plotinus and Saint Augustine, were both of North African origin.

Christian Metaphysics and Neoplatonism is divided into four chapters representing the four stages seen by Camus as defining the development of Christianity. The first, "Evangelical Christianity," views the Gospels as essentially conceiving of the new religion in terms of revelatory faith without reference to any philosophical motifs. Next comes "Gnosis," in which innovative Christian trends mingle with those of Greece; gnosticism is the result in which, even while God remains ineffable, salvation becomes attainable and thereby intertwined with a certain idea of knowing. The third chapter, "Mystical Reason," deals with Neoplatonism and its crucial impact on Christianity. Plotinus, who founded this philosophical movement in the third century, is the main focus of attention. His belief in a cosmological connection between God and the world understands the divine as intelligible even as truth and beauty are fused in a contemplative vision of paradise. "Feeling is on the alert for new discoveries," and Camus finds in Plotinus "a certain tragedy in that effort to pour emotion into the logical forms of Greek idealism."[16] The result, however, is ultimately a set of "ready-made formulas" with which Saint Augustine later created a full-blown Christian metaphysic predicated on original sin and the possibilities of grace.

The historical aim of the study was to contest the mechanical view of Christianity as the simple successor to classical culture (*Christian Metaphysics*, 96). Its philosophic purpose was actually threefold: it suggested that Greek philosophy turned Christianity against nature by orienting it toward metaphysics; it emphasized the particular importance of Neoplatonism for Christianity; and, finally, it obviously called on readers to reconsider the rigid divorce between reason and revelation, or the "pagan" and the "civilized." The conclusion challenges the common view that Hellenism conquered Christianity; instead, Christianity absorbs Hellenism. As later with his own views on ethics, Camus could claim: "Christian morality cannot be taught; it is an interior ascesis which serves to ratify a faith" (*Christian Metaphysics*, 151).

Camus would never employ the classical legacy in the manner of important contemporary political theorists like Hannah Arendt or Eric Vogelin. He was unconcerned with the *polis* as an ideal or politics as a form of "self-exhibition," in the manner of Arendt. He similarly never conceived the religious world as maintaining a coherence or a set of moral standards by which the degeneration of modernity might be judged, in the manner of Vogelin.

16. Albert Camus, *Christian Metaphysics and Neoplatonism*, in McBride, *Albert Camus*, 125. Subsequent page references to this work appear parenthetically in the text.

Camus emerged from his dissertation neither as a Platonist nor as an Augustinian, although many of their themes would remain with him, but with a Pelagian belief in the centrality of the individual in determining his or her destiny.[17]

The classical legacy would inform the more existential and phenomenological characteristics of Camus's later work. Neoplatonism already evinces what would become his disdain for rigidly separating reason from emotion and his dislike for all systems: morality also already takes precedence over any codified ethics. Camus would find his own way of putting "feeling on the alert," and he, too, would employ language to convey the most deeply personal forms of experience. Plotinus had originally seen language as a way of clarifying religious revelation that basic insight was embraced by Saint Augustine in his *Confessions.* This was probably the first self-conscious autobiography, and in its pages Camus saw the possibility of personal experience becoming a constant point of reference for a literary and philosophical undertaking. In fact, just as with Camus, the two genres merge in this great work of Saint Augustine.

The *Confessions,* obviously fueled by intense reflection, also assumed a natural feeling, propensity, or desire for God on the part of every person. Even though Camus already considered himself an atheist when he wrote *Christian Metaphysics and Neoplatonism,* he would make the most of this idea: the absence of God would become coupled with the longing for salvation and meaning only He could provide. This paradoxical situation would profoundly influence all of Camus's future writings. It in-

17. Todd, *Albert Camus,* 105.

forms what he would call the "absurd" character of existence and also holds the key to the problem of his religiosity, which has generated intense debate and has usually
been misconstrued.[18]

Camus was neither a closet Catholic nor a secular
thinker who, like Voltaire, considered religion little more
than "superstition." His secular standpoint was determined by the religious faith he opposed and, in this regard, he was actually representative of a general philosophical trend commonly known as "religious atheism."
Its philosophical proponents, such as Friedrich Nietzsche,
Martin Heidegger, and Karl Jaspers, were all radical indi-
vidualists and sophisticated intellectuals. Whatever their
youthful concerns or their political passions, as mature
thinkers they belonged to no church, embraced no form
of religious dogma, and founded no mass movement.

All of them emphasized the role of personal experience and the responsibility of the individual in shaping
his or her fate. All also sought to counter the "emptiness" of modern philosophical traditions like idealism
and materialism. Religious atheism gave expression to
the inner poverty caused by modern science and com-
modity production, or what Max Weber termed the

18. Influential trends and the implications generated by basic philosophical assumptions are generally ignored in the debate concerning
the religious or secular character of Camus's thought. Note the articles
by Thomas L. Hannah, "Albert Camus and the Christian Faith"; Bernard
C. Murchland, C.S.C., "Albert Camus: The Dark Night before the
Coming of Grace?"; and Henri Peyre, "Camus the Pagan," all of which
are included in *Camus: A Collection of Critical Essays*, ed. Germaine Brée
(Englewood, N.J., 1962), 48–70. Also note the studies by Jean Onimus,
Albert Camus and Christianity, trans. Emmett Parker (Tuscaloosa,
1970), and Joseph Hermet, *Albert Camus et Le Christianisme: L'espérance
en procès* (Paris, 1976).

"disenchantment of the world." This general trend informs the search for spiritual foundations in the paintings of Kandinsky, the music of Schoenberg, and the work of modernist movements like expressionism. Indeed, even if many of religious atheism's major representatives were atheists or agnostics, God became the point of philosophical reference.

Camus would formulate his philosophy in these terms. The "absurd" can exist only if God is absent. But this means issues of religion have been taken seriously in the first place. Camus's preoccupation with an absolute, whether with respect to its existence or merely the longing for its existence, provided the context for investigating new problems of both an existential and a political nature. The point is rarely taken seriously enough: no less than with the leading figures of existentialist philosophy and avant-garde culture, Camus would also find himself defined by what he opposed with respect to religion.

EXPERIMENTS

A Happy Death was the first sustained literary effort of Camus. Its title inverted that of *The Happy Life,* the first philosophical effort of Saint Augustine, and—with bitter irony—its message sought to contest the old saying "money can't buy happiness." The book was written around 1937, when Camus was working as a journalist and again performing odd jobs, but was not published until 1971. Its hero, Patrice Mersault, suffers from tuberculosis. He evinces a certain lassitude and indifference toward existence. He is driven to self-conscious action only when his former teacher, a legless cripple named Zagreus, complains of being forced to await a "natural death"; indeed, from the name and the description of the action, Camus conjures the image of an assault on Zeus or a veiled reference to what Nietzsche termed "the death of God."

Repulsed by the fate in store for his former mentor, and tempted by his money, Mersault shoots Zagreus, makes the murder look like suicide, and robs him in the hope of securing a happy life. Camus was obviously seeking to work through the central premise or contradiction of Saint Augustine's *The Happy Life,* in which it becomes apparent that, though no one can be happy who lacks what he or she desires, a person may have what is desired and still not be happy. Saint Augustine seeks to emphasize the primacy of grace against the search for truth or the delight in experiencing earthly pleasure; Camus wants to argue the opposite. But he is not quite certain which way to proceed and, following the murder, the story begins to disintegrate.

Mersault wanders through central Europe, but the grayness depresses him. He longs for the sun and returns to Algiers, where he happily shares a residence (remarkably similar to the House at the Edge of the World) with three young women, and marries another. In the end, unrepentant, Mersault dies of tuberculosis. A certain "pagan" sensualism becomes the response to a fallen and decadent Christian world in *A Happy Death.* There is no salvation and no "tomorrow." There are experiences of joy. Even the beauty of nature cannot compensate for the existence of injustice or the certainty of death.[19]

A parallel emerges with *The Stranger,* for which *A Happy Death* served as a dress rehearsal. Its hero shows

---

19. Thus, while visiting the Cemetery of El Kettar, Camus noted: "One solitary geranium, its leaves both pink and red, and a great silent feeling of loss and sadness that teaches us to know the pure and beautiful face of death" (Camus, *Notebooks,* 1: 74).

marked similarities to and has virtually the identical name as the protagonist of the later work. Both novels are set in Algeria and deal with similar themes. A murder takes place in both, though in *A Happy Death* Zagreus rather than a nameless Arab is the victim. Both novels oscillate between pessimism and optimism, as Camus did himself. Just like his atheism, which took shape in opposition to Catholicism, each of these two mutually exclusive views of life became defined by the other. Indeed, this also occurred in the two collections of essays written around the same time as *A Happy Death.*

"The Wrong Side and the Right Side" was published in a limited edition in 1937 by Charlot, a small publishing house, and *Nuptials* appeared two years later. It was only with great hesitancy that Camus consented to republish them in 1958. He was ostensibly concerned about their lack of craft and the clumsiness of expression in certain of the essays. But he must also have been somewhat ambivalent about their autobiographical character; indeed, the 1958 preface to "The Wrong Side and the Right Side" noted: "Here are my people, my teachers, my ancestry; here is what, through them, links me with everyone" (*Lyrical and Critical Essays,* 14).

Following Grenier, each of the collections is constructed around diffuse and immediate impressions of reality. But the whole is still more than the sum of its parts. Various essays such as "Between Yes and No" exhibit a somewhat self-pitying and emotionally effusive quality foreign to the more mature works, while others, like "Summer in Algiers," tend to romanticize working-class life. At their best, these sketches of momentary experiences and everyday life combine an effusively sensual content with an austere and pristine form for which Camus would become known. They certainly provide an antidote to the apocalyptic tone and bitter world-weariness common to so many of the writings of the 1920s and 1930s. The essays' unaffected embrace of nature and their rejection of psychological extremism, their mixture of sensuality with a quiet, meditative quality, and, above all, their genuine biculturalism contribute to their uniqueness.

Both collections express the same tension. Outside is the sun, the sea, and physical experience. Inside is isolation, bitter poverty, cramped quarters, and a peculiar, stultifying silence. Camus stands "betwixt and between," slipping from the one into the other, flipping the two sides of the cloth back and forth, as the title of the first collection, *L'Envers et L'endroit,* suggests. Pessimism and optimism are operative in both collections. Camus believed that neither can ever abolish the other. These essays already make clear how "lucidity," in Camus's view, calls for remaining aware of the tension between opposing attitudes and preserving a sense of balance.

Pessimism dominates "The Wrong Side and the Right Side." A bitter observation, "death for us all, but his own death to each," unifies its essays (*Lyrical and Critical Essays,* 29). Camus felt a profound sadness in Prague, where he had gone on holiday with Simone and a close friend, Yves Bourgeois, only to suffer his two companions' running off together. The moments of joy are outweighed by this experience, which actually marked the final break in Camus's marriage, along with descriptions of illness and a growing sense of the contingency of existence. Following the completion of this essay collection, in fact, Camus experienced his first bout of writer's block (*Lyrical and Critical Essays,* 358). He confronted the darkness in *Nuptials,* which is marked by a radical sensualism. It highlights the wedding of man and earth as well as the rejection of sin and religion. There, in "The Winds at Djemila," Camus wrote: "I think of flowers, smiles, the desire for women, and realize that my whole horror of death lies in my anxiety to live" (*Lyrical and Critical Essays,* 78).

Considering the two works in relation to each other makes it clear how, for Camus, the contingency of existence creates the impulse for affirming it. Insofar as optimism lacks any form of absolute justification, it can only exist in momentary eruptions. It will then give way again to pessimism. The pessimism of the earlier collection and the optimism of the later affirm one another. Both works also evince the tension between a "Western" interpretive quest for meaning and a "Mediterranean" emphasis on physical reality—"the sea, sun, and women in the light"—of which Camus would speak in his introductory editorial for the short-lived literary magazine for Mediterranean culture, *Rivages,* which he began editing in 1938.

There is perhaps something stereotypical about the ways in which the words "Western" and "Mediterranean" are used both by Camus and most of his interpreters. But the tension between them in these essays is as manifest as that between pessimism and optimism. In neither case is there a possibility for progress or regression. We arbitrarily sway back and forth on the waves of opposing attitudes. We can only balance the one with the other as best we can. "The Desert," the last essay of *Nuptials,* makes this clear:

> It is on this moment of balance I must end: the strange moment when spirituality rejects ethics, when happiness springs from the absence of hope, when the mind finds its justification in the body. If it is true that every truth carries its bitterness within, it

is also true that every denial contains a flourish of affirmations. (*Lyrical and Critical Essays,* 104)

ACTIVISM

The 1930s was a decade of powerful personalities: Churchill, Hitler, Mussolini, Roosevelt, Stalin. It was culturally rich. It was dramatic. It was also a decade that, outside of the United States, was primarily marked by counter-revolution. The economic depression of 1929 spread over a continent still reeling from World War I and its aftershocks. Certain republics, which had arisen in the 1920s, collapsed under its weight and the rest trembled. Stalinism had replaced the vague, if radically democratic, hopes expressed by the "Soviets" during the "heroic years" of the Russian Revolution, and fascism seemed to incarnate the future during the 1930s.

The authoritarian precursors of the Nazis had already triumphed in Hungary in 1919, Poland in 1920, and the Baltic states. The year 1921 saw Benito Mussolini take power in Italy, more than a decade before the Nazis finally overthrew what remained of the ill-fated Weimar Republic in 1933. Fascism blossomed in Austria and Finland. Its supporters in France mostly clustered around the Action Française, a dangerous mass movement far larger than German National Socialism during the 1920s, while a significant minority joined smaller if even more violent organizations.

Fascism became an international phenomenon. Everywhere its opponents appeared divided and on the defensive. Liberalism had never developed a mass base in Europe; its political representatives were identified with free-market capitalism and the interests of big business.

Social democracy, which was embraced by the majority of workers, mixed a commitment to economic reform with support for republican regimes of Europe in the postwar period; its representatives, however, were staunchly legalistic in their attitudes and seemingly lacked the will to fight in those states where fascism proved triumphant. As for communism, it was embraced only by a radical minority of the European working class, and its politics was dangerously sectarian. Isolated by the capitalist world, intent upon world revolution, the Soviet Union had already refused support for endangered "bourgeois" republican regimes in 1923, and Stalin went even further in 1928 by identifying social democrats as "twin brothers" of the fascists. Nevertheless, this disciplined and ideologically militant movement at least appeared willing to engage the fascist enemy.

Camus made the same choice as many committed young antifascists of his generation even if he was somewhat eclectic in his beliefs. During 1931 and 1932, Gustave Acault had introduced him to anarchist ideas, with which the young nonconformist, who knew poverty so well, showed a certain sympathy, and Jean Grenier spoke to him of revolutionary syndicalism. Camus would maintain his interest in anarcho-syndicalism until the end of his life.[20] But even as a young man, Camus was never a sectarian. For a time, he worked with Max-Pol Fouchet and the Young Socialists, though, of course, this became increasingly difficult given the personal problems between them. Other ideas were at work, however, different from the determinism inspiring the original social democratic labor

20. Ian Birchall, "The Labourism of Sisyphus: Albert Camus and Revolutionary Syndicalism," *Journal of European Studies* 20 (1992): 135 ff.

movement and the bureaucratic dogmatism increasingly dominating the Communist International. Camus was profoundly affected by the vision of communism as a new form of "fraternity," the hero as the "new man" willing to face death for the sake of his comrades, and politics as an incarnation of the "extreme situation." These were the views elaborated by André Malraux in his sensational novel *Man's Fate*. As political events began to unfold in 1934, they were seemingly justified by a new sense of political urgency.

Camus made his choice. With the support of Grenier, who falsely believed a small group of intelligent people could positively influence a relatively weak if disciplined organization, the young man entered the Communist Party in Algeria. A romantic aura fostered by a cadre of intellectuals and propagandists surrounded the movement. Camus ignored what was essential about Stalin and rendered general homages to Lenin. Nevertheless, politically and ideologically, Camus had his doubts from the beginning. He jotted into his notebooks:

> Grenier on Communism: "The whole question comes down to this: should one, for an ideal of justice, accept stupid ideas?" One can reply "yes," this is a fine thing to do. Or "no," it is honest to refuse.[21]

Camus was never a Marxist with respect to matters of theory, and undoubtedly, communism was little more than an instrument for realizing his vague hopes for a better world.[22] It is still not certain exactly when Camus joined the Communist Party or even how long he remained a member. It is certain that he recruited Jeanne-Paul Sicard

21. Camus, *Notebooks*, 1: 16.
22. Todd, *Albert Camus*, 87.

and Marguerite Dobrenn. He later tried to downplay his association during those years in which purges were claiming the lives of millions in the Soviet Union. Most probably, however, Camus entered in either 1934 or 1935 and remained a member until 1937.[23]

There was a certain justification for his decision to join the party. The Soviet Union was the homeland of the proletarian revolution. It was seemingly the sole supporter of anti-imperialist struggles in colonized lands like Algeria. Its propaganda reflected the concerns of the disempowered and disenfranchised, with whom Camus had lived since his childhood. It also appeared by late 1934 as if the communists might soon abandon their sectarian policy.

The year 1933 witnessed the formation of the Congress against War and Fascism by pacifist writers such as Romain Rolland and Henri Barbusse, and by 1934 the need for unity seemed even more urgent as fascist rioting shook France. Socialists and communists quickly responded with a pact pledging mutual support in the antifascist struggle. Their unions followed suit. A French Committee of Antifascist Intellectuals was founded in 1934, and then, early in 1935, an International Conference for the Defense of Culture took place. Malraux and Gide, who sympathized with the French Communist Party, took part along with a host of other intellectual luminaries in what would become a legendary event.[24] Then, finally, on July 14, 1935,

23. McCarthy, *Camus*, 55; Guérin, *Camus*, 16. Other scholars claim that Camus entered the Communist Party in 1934, and the least critical claim, or suggest that he left a year later. Cf. Philip Thody, *Albert Camus 1913–1960* (London, 1961), 5; Brée, *Camus*, 26; also, Lottman, *Albert Camus*, 77 ff. The best discussion of Camus's time in the party, and his expulsion, is offered by Todd, *Albert Camus*, 134 ff.

24. Stephen Eric Bronner, "Political Aesthetics in Retrospect," *Of Critical Theory and Its Theorists* (London, 1994), 155 ff.

the day commemorating the fall of the Bastille in 1789, antifascists from all the major parties came together, and in a demonstration 500,000 strong in Paris, declared their intention to act as a "Popular Front."[25]

The Popular Front scored a remarkable victory in the elections of 1936, and its radical program of social and economic reforms laid the basis for the modern French welfare state. The tenure of this antifascist coalition was brief: the Popular Front was defeated in 1937 and only ruled again for a few months during 1938. But it solidified the connection between liberalism and socialism. The Popular Front abolished the sectarianism of the 1920s and inspired a new ethos of humanism and solidarity in any number of famous films and novels, ranging from *The Grand Illusion* by Jean Renoir to *The Seventh Cross* by Anna Seghers. Above all, the Popular Front gave hope to millions. An apparently viable political strategy had, finally, been found to counter the spread of fascism.[26]

Nowhere was the implementation of this strategy seemingly more imperative than in Spain. A republic had been created in 1931, but it never won the heart of the Catholic church, the military, the aristocracy, or any of those other groups that had supported fascist movements elsewhere in Europe. Under the leadership of General Francisco Franco, with promises of support from Hitler

25. A month later, with Georgi Dimitrov of Bulgaria and Palmiero Togliatti of Italy taking leading roles, the Seventh Congress of the Communist International formally ratified what had already taken place. Cf. E. H. Carr, *Twilight of the Comintern: 1930–1935*, ed. Tamara Deutscher (New York, 1982), 403 ff.

26. A more complete analysis is provided in the chapter "Léon Blum and the Legacy of the Popular Front," in Stephen Eric Bronner, *Moments of Decision: Political History and the Crises of Radicalism* (New York, 1992), 57 ff.

and Mussolini, the Spanish army staged a revolt in 1936. This action sparked what would become a horrible civil war. Anarchists, communists, liberals, socialists, and Trotskyists responded by joining together to defend the republic in a Spanish version of the Popular Front.

Conflicts over economic policy, politics, and foreign policy quickly undermined the Popular Front in France. These conflicts took an even more disastrous form in Spain. Anarchists and Trotskyists, who wished to carry forward a revolution while fighting the civil war, found themselves confronting a coalition of communists, social democrats, and bourgeois republicans who all opposed such radicalism for different reasons. This intractable division within the antifascist camp soon led to violence. With the communists in command, in 1937 the anarchist revolutionaries were massacred at the Battle of Barcelona, sealing the fascist victory. The internecine hatreds existing in the antifascist movement had proven disastrous. Nevertheless, the Spanish civil war immediately became a symbol of revolutionary valor and antifascist resistance.[27]

The Spanish civil war would symbolically remain with Camus until the end of his life. He was, from the first, swept away like so many others of his generation.[28] André Malraux published an underrated novel about the conflict,

27. For differing interpretations, see Barnett Bolloten, *The Spanish Revolution: The Left and the Struggle for Power during the Civil War* (Chapel Hill, 1979); Franz Borkenau, *The Spanish Cockpit* (Ann Arbor, 1963); George Orwell, *Homage to Catalonia* (London, 1939); Henry Pachter, *Espagne 1936–7: La guerre devore la révolution* (Paris, 1986).

28. "The left-wing press gave it so wide a coverage that it might have been a French affair—and in effect it was: at all costs we had to prevent yet another Fascist state from establishing itself on our borders." Simone de Beauvoir, *The Prime of Life,* trans. Peter Green (New York, 1973), 332.

which was translated as *Man's Hope,* and Ernest Hemingway wrote *For Whom the Bell Tolls;* George Orwell initially made his reputation with *Homage to Catalonia,* and Bertolt Brecht was inspired to write *The Rifles of Mother Carrar.* Camus contributed to the ideological struggle in 1936 with the avant-garde play *Revolt in the Asturias,* which identified with an uprising of anarchist Spanish miners in 1934.[29] But he was also supportive of the antifascist coalition in which the communists played an important role. Camus never came to terms with the causes for the defeat of the loyalists.

The Spanish civil war provides the first and most dramatic example of what would become his tendency to view politics in primarily symbolic terms. He was, from the beginning, less interested in questions of political power than the symbolism evoked by major events and the normative values at stake. This was certainly the case during his time in the Communist Party. His motivations were never really those of the movement, even if his cultural activity in projects like *Revolt in the Asturias,* along with his public speaking on significant issues, made him one of its best-known militants.[30]

Disillusionment came soon enough. Its initial source was a seemingly innocuous invitation extended by Stalin to Pierre Laval in 1935. A minister in various conservative governments, an archreactionary, Laval would later lead the fascist vassal-state of Vichy following the defeat of France in 1940. The invitation from Stalin was clearly a friendly gesture to the French Right. Changing course from his sectarian line of 1928, which had equated socialists

29. Todd, *Albert Camus,* 124.
30. Lottman, *Albert Camus,* 147.

with Nazis and helped bring about the triumph of Hitler, he now sought to embrace all possible allies in the antifascist cause. Stalin was also willing to pay a price. Even while preparing for the Popular Front, he insisted that the communists sever their connection with the Algerian liberation struggle.

Camus initially opposed inclusion of more conservative antifascists in the Popular Front. He undoubtedly anticipated the break they would attempt to impose on its economic policies even if he underestimated the difficulty of winning an election without them. He also stood in the forefront of communists willing to work with Algerian nationalists and was a prominent advocate of the bill initiated by Léon Blum and Maurice Viollette, the socialist leader of the Popular Front and his minister of state, which would extend voting rights to 200,000 Muslims. The prospect of its passage resulted in raucous demonstrations by French settlers and, in keeping with his resolution, Stalin called on communists to retract their support. Camus balked. Even worse, he broke the fundamental rule underlying what the communists called "democratic centralism" by taking his criticisms outside the confines of the organization. He was expelled, supposedly in 1937, and quickly broke all ties with the communist movement.

Camus stood by his friends and refused to renounce the democratic principles on which the Popular Front, if not communist interests, was based. But it was clear from the first that the Blum-Viollette bill would never reach the floor of the French Parliament. It was also obvious that the new and less strident policy of the Communist Party on Algeria was tactical and of little real importance, given its meager size. As far as the Laval visit was concerned, its actual pur-

pose was to provide Stalin the opportunity to communicate his support for a rearmament of France in the face of a
growing Nazi threat.[31] Indeed, this decision allowed the
French communists to embrace patriotism openly.

But Camus was never a nationalist. He was a pacifist
and also an advocate of what the British prime minister,
Neville Chamberlain, called "appeasement." This policy
was predicated on the assumption that the territorial ambitions of fascist states, including Nazi Germany, were
limited, and its aim was to avoid war at all costs. The cow-
ardice and arrogance, the inhuman indifference to the victims of fascism and the antifascist cause in the name of
peace and an ill-informed sense of Realpolitik, never came
into play. Sartre would later highlight this in *The Reprieve.*
Given the still-fresh memory of World War I, however, appeasement was not quite as absurd a policy as it may now
appear. Many brave and honorable people during the
1920s and 1930s, among all moderate and left-wing parties,
could join in the cry: "Never Again War!"

The strategy began wearing thin by 1936 as the scope of

31. The communists believed that "to beat fascism it was essential to
prevent it from winning recruits from the middle classes, who had assured its success wherever it had attained power . . . The middle class
radicals to whom the communists were now appealing were antago-
nized by Laval's economic policy. His visit to Moscow was marked on 15
May 1935 by a celebrated episode. In their joint communique Laval ob-
tained from Stalin a statement of his understanding and approval of
'the policy of national defense pursued by France in keeping her armed
forces at the level needed for her security.' Laval's aim, cunning rather
than clever, was to embarrass the French communists by making their
anti-militarism look absurd in the light of the Russians' need for a pact
with France against German foreign policy. Contrary to expectations,
this in fact made it easier for the communists to express wholehearted
patriotism." Philippe Bernard and Henri Dubief, *The Decline of the
Third Republic, 1914–38,* trans. Anthony Forster (New York, 1988), 295.

fascist domination increased. Japan conquered Manchuria; the world stood by. Italy invaded Abyssinia; Abyssinia's small and valiant army received no assistance. Germany began rearming in 1934, marched into the Rhineland in 1936, and annexed Austria in 1938. Each time Hitler threatened war, and each time France and England backed down. Then, also in 1938, he called for severing the Sudetenland from the Republic of Czechoslovakia and integrating it into Germany. This, he swore, would constitute his last territorial demand.

Edouard Daladier of France, Chamberlain, and Mussolini met with Hitler in Munich. Czechoslovakia played no role in the negotiations between its avowed enemies and the Western democracies with which it was formally allied. England and France cynically agreed to Hitler's demand for what would amount to the dismemberment of Czechoslovakia in exchange for a short-lived peace. Camus supported the Munich Pact of 1938, which was perhaps understandable. Incomprehensible, however, was his continuing support for the policy of "appeasement" even after Hitler swallowed the remainder of Czechoslovakia and Winston Churchill replaced Chamberlain. The Nazis attacked Poland in 1939, beginning World War II. Camus tried to enlist in solidarity, but he was rejected for health reasons. Nevertheless, he continued to call upon the Allies to negotiate.[32]

32. Given the circumstances, it is somewhat of an exaggeration to claim that "Politically, Camus' view was ridiculous. Despite his antifascist stand, he had not grasped the nature of the Hitler regime. Not until after the Fall of France did he realize that it was especially virulent. Moreover, he chose to ignore that France could not fight Hitler while parading her readiness to negotiate with him. While insisting that he was rejecting fatalism in the name of action, Camus was condemning himself to passivity." McCarthy, *Camus*, 125.

At this time Camus was earning his living as a journalist. In 1938 he had met Pascal Pia, who appointed him to the staff of *Algér-Républicain.* Born in 1901, orphaned by the war, and poor, Pia had entered bohemian circles at a young age. There he met the surrealist poet Louis Aragon, who would later become an orthodox communist, and André Malraux, with whom he became particularly close. Pia had been at the center of numerous scandals, including one in which he published erotic writings in the familiar pink covers of a well-known series of children's books, before becoming a newspaperman and deciding to run the new daily in Algiers. An anarchist and devotee of surrealism, Pia chose to remain in the background and work for the glory of his more talented friends. This he did for Malraux and Aragon, and also for Camus.[33]

Pia taught Camus the journalistic craft. He took Camus along on the rounds of police stations, law courts, and city council sessions. He supported his younger friend, who, without concern for a correct political "line," began publishing literary reviews of "living works" by relatively unknown young writers like Jean-Paul Sartre and Jean Giraudoux. Under the tutelage of Pia, however, Camus primarily turned his attention to political matters. He wrote articles supporting the Spanish Republic, attacking attempts to roll back the reforms of the Popular Front, and criticizing the Treaty of Versailles for the burdens it placed on Germany in the aftermath of World War I. He also defended innocent victims of colonial injustice and police torture in Algeria by noting "when abject methods succeed in leading to the penal colony unhappy men whose life had already been only a series of miseries, then

33. Todd, *Albert Camus,* 174 ff.; Lottman, *Albert Camus,* 186 ff.

it represents for each of us a kind of personal injury that is impossible to accept."

His gripping editorials exposing incompetence and seeking European aid during the terrible Kabylian famine of 1939 created a sensation in Algiers and turned him into something of a celebrity. For the moment, however, his fame was fleeting. *Algér-Républicain* was closed down during 1939 and, ironically, Camus found that his political interventions had made him unemployable.[34] When Pia secured him a job as a reporter with *Paris Soir* early in 1940, he decided to leave Algiers for France.

Upon arriving, he soon became profoundly depressed. He barely knew anyone there. He loathed working for this conservative mass-market paper, owned by Jean Prouvoust, who would later join the Vichy government, which was fundamentally preoccupied with crime, film stars, and scandal. Adding to his depression was the gray gloom of the city, the cheap hotels, the grinding poverty, and his separation from his second wife, Francine Faure, whom he had just married.

There was also the war. Camus essentially saw the conflict as a product of human error and blindness[35]—a simplistic stance born of moralism and political immaturity. But it didn't hurt his work. Those dark times inspired a new notion of the absurd and three of its most dramatic representatives: Meursault, Sisyphus, and Caligula.

34. Justin O'Brien, "Albert Camus: Militant," *Camus,* ed. Brée, 23.
35. Brée, *Camus,* 35.

2 — the absurd

"The three absurds," Camus could note in his journal entry of February 21, 1941, "are now complete."[1] He was speaking about *The Stranger, The Myth of Sisyphus,* and *Caligula.* The first is a novel, the second an essay, and the third a play. Together they represent the literary range of Camus. The three were written around the same time, and, in his mind, they became linked by a word: the absurd. Of these three works, *The Stranger* is the best known. Finished in 1940, it did not appear until 1942. Finding a publisher was not easy. Camus was still virtually unknown in France, and, supposedly, André Malraux "imposed" the novel on the major French publisher Gallimard.[2] It is now viewed as a classic. Few such genuinely enigmatic works, which distance even while they emotionally engage the reader, have ever had this kind of success. Perhaps it seduces with its strange egoism. It was surely considered new in its style. Although it is rarely considered this way, however, it

1. Camus, *Notebooks,* 1: 189.
2. Thody, *Albert Camus,* 29.

31

actually presents a modern form of the "educational novel" (bildungsroman).

The Stranger fuses the modernism of André Malraux and the classical prose of André Gide with an exoticism both often shared in their writings. The detachment of its author and main character also owes much to American authors like Ernest Hemingway and James Cain. But it doesn't intentionally celebrate cynicism, nihilism, or the loss of values—quite the contrary. Its close is a celebration of the lived life, and the novel deals with the transformation of an indifferent yet self-absorbed individual, a man committed to remaking his life in the shadow of death.

Meursault, the main character, initially appears disinterested in anything other than immediate physical sensations and honesty. He doesn't care about money or promotions and displays no emotions when his mother dies. He expresses no feelings at her funeral, other than discomfort in the heat, but he notices the most incidental objects like the screws in the coffin and the clothes people are wearing. The day of the funeral is a day like any other, and on the morrow he goes swimming, where he meets a young girl whom he seduces and then takes as his mistress. Maria Cardona, who bears the name of Camus's grandmother, asks him to marry her and he agrees. Meursault is polite but remains emotionally distant.

One choice is as meaningless as the next and encounter follows encounter. Meursault goes again to the beach with his fiancée and his friend Raymond Sintes, whose last name echoes that of Camus's mother, along with Sintes's girlfriend. He says nothing when his friend beats his girlfriend. They chance upon a group of Arabs, who have a score to settle with Sintes, a pimp and a tough. Words are exchanged, the men scuffle, then everyone disperses.

Blinded by the sun and looking for a spot of shade, however, Meursault returns and meets one of the Arabs, who flashes a knife. Meursault fires a shot, then four more. The Arab lies dead. The police arrest Meursault. He is put on trial and condemned to death. But the reason for this extreme judgment has little to do with the murder. In Algeria, with the racist attitudes of the French colonial administration, such an act would normally receive only a few years of imprisonment. The real reason the jury condemns Meursault stems from his refusal, under cross-examination, to explain his actions or to lie about his inability to weep at his mother's funeral. This "stranger" from himself and society now waits for death. In prison, Meursault makes use of his memories and forgets the boredom that had defined his previous existence. The chaplain comes and is turned away.

Camus had already written in his notebooks, in 1935 and 1936, that he was considering composing a story about a "man who refuses to justify himself."[3] *A Happy Death* is that story, but his new character, Meursault, is that man. Society must elicit a reason for his actions, and since he refuses to provide one, the prosecutor portrays him as a cold-blooded psychopath. In fact, his act of murder is neither more nor less arbitrary than any of his other more human experiences. Camus takes great pains to show that there is no objective answer for *why* Meursault killed the Arab. It was a "gratuitous act," an act without reason or justification, which incidentally has its own literary tradition in Dostoyevsky, Gide, Malraux, the surrealists, and others. The act without purpose indeed mirrors a world without meaning.

3. Camus, *Notebooks*, 1: 32.

The Stranger is concerned with the creation of meaning in a meaningless world. Society offers no answers. Its hypocritical moralism is reflected in the trial of Meursault where a "divorce" occurs between the objective and subjective reasons for the judgment offered by the jury. Meursault is innocent of the crimes for which he is actually sentenced and guilty of what is essentially ignored. An irresolvable paradox exists between the objective judgment of an action and the subjective motivations behind its performance. Truth disappears. Therein lies the absurdity of existence. But where this same paradox generated anxiety and an impulse toward faith for Søren Kierkegaard, the nineteenth-century Danish philosopher who first introduced the concept of the absurd and is generally considered the founder of existentialism, it produced in Camus a proud and personal rebellion against the incoherence of existence.[4]

Meursault never gave meaning to his actions or his life, but in prison he tries, and memory allows him to do so. Memory was a dominant motif for major writers of the previous generation, such as Marcel Proust and James Joyce. Memory awakens Meursault's sense of responsibility and enables him to reappropriate his life. *The Stranger* becomes less a testament to the absurdity of life than a reaction against it, a modern form of the educational novel.

Meursault is sunk in the absurd as the novel begins. He is passive, unreflective, and compulsive. At stake is the way in which he loses his feelings of apathy and indifference and uses his memory in order to regain a sense of the pre-

4. Søren Kierkegaard, *Fear and Trembling,* trans. Walter Lowrie (Princeton, 1941), 43 ff. Regarding Camus, Jean-Paul Sartre, "An Explication of *The Stranger,*" in *Camus,* ed. Brée, 108 ff.

cious quality of his life. Meursault is not an intellectual, which makes him different from other characters of a similar type, such as the introspective Roquentin in *Nausea* by Jean-Paul Sartre. Instead, he is a semiproletarian who "exists entirely in the present."[5] Given the street tough he represents, his apathy and self-absorption, it would have been out of character for him to have expressed outrage when his friend beat up his girlfriend or to have told the truth about this incident to the police. Criticism in this regard is misdirected and ignores the developmental character of the work: a person like Meursault, certainly at that point in the novel, does not squeal on his friends.[6] In his own way, Meursault prizes honesty. Thus, Camus could write:

> The hero of my book is condemned because he does not play the game . . . [H]e refuses to lie . . . [and] one would therefore not be much mistaken to read *The Stranger* as the story of a man who, without any heroics, agrees to die for the truth. I also happened to say, again paradoxically, that I had tried to draw in my character the only Christ we deserve.[7]

Meursault's honesty makes it possible for him to change as the novel progresses. He learns to overcome the "habit" of living, as well as the indifference and relativism of an "absurd" existence, by assuming responsibility for his life. His refusal of communion and metaphysical hope occurs in the name of a new appreciation of physical life with its

5. Quilliot, *The Sea and Prisons*, 70.

6. O'Brien, *Albert Camus of Europe and Africa*, 20 ff.

7. Camus, "Preface to *The Stranger* (1955)," in *Lyrical and Critical Essays*, 336–37.

here and now.[8] Meursault becomes his own person. The closing pages of *The Stranger,* with the beautiful evocation of physical existence and the richness of life, provide a sense of the "lucidity" experienced by this murderer awaiting death. Indeed, just before his execution, Meursault can feel himself

> ready to start life all over again. It was as if that great rush of anger had washed me clean, emptied me of hope and, gazing up at the dark sky spangled with its signs and stars, for the first time, the first, I laid my heart open to the benign indifference of the universe. To feel it so like myself, indeed, so brotherly, made me realize that I'd been happy and that I was happy still. [9]

Sartre saw *The Stranger* as a novel "about the absurd and against the absurd."[10] It offers a penetrating critique of the death penalty and "the world of the trial." But the possibility of judgment becomes tenuous. Not only does the novel say nothing about the concrete situation in Algeria, but it threatens to leave the reader adrift in the relativism its author claims to reject. The question is whether this is a weakness or a strength—a mistake in construction or a vigorous invitation for self-reflection.

Camus understood *The Stranger* as the "story of a man who, without any heroics, agrees to die for the truth."

---

8. "What the priest attempts to do, in Meursault's eyes, is to steal from him that life which has become his good in the face of death, to take away the value which has revealed itself against the background of death." Robert J. Champigny, *A Pagan Hero: An Interpretation of Meursault in Camus' "The Stranger,"* trans. Rowe Portis (Philadelphia, 1969), 95.

9. Camus, *The Stranger,* 154.

10. Sartre, "An Explication of *The Stranger,*" 114.

Meursault refuses any form of illusory hope even as he strives to contest the absurd. He is, in this respect, authentic. But what of the act and its implications for those other than himself? What of the friends and family of the Arab? The novel never explicitly denies the need for a moral form of social conduct, which would increasingly concern Camus as he grew older, but it clearly highlights a bohemian individualism that the author would never fully relinquish.[11] The conflict between them remains, and as a consequence Meursault becomes both an exemplary and a cautionary figure.

Critics have often seen this as a deficiency,[12] and perhaps Camus's refusal to resolve the motivations of his main character—or "make matters clear"—adds to its difficulty. Again, it remains an open question whether this is a weakness or a strength: an abdication of responsibility or a recognition of ambiguity. The crucial point is usually missed precisely because Camus's connection with existentialism is underestimated: Camus no less than most existentialists considered such conflicts between subjective intention and objective judgments philosophically irresolvable and all universal solutions inherently abstract. His understanding of the character is therefore tied to his general philosophical position and, from his own perspective, the internal needs of the work.

The Stranger was never meant to offer a rigorous ethics. The experience of Meursault is unique and untranslatable. His response to the absurd is closed to codification. The coherent moral stance of the novel must necessarily prove unsystematic from the standpoint of philosophy. This

11. Pierre-Georges Castex, *Albert Camus et 'L'Etranger'* (Paris, 1965), 123.

12. Thody, *Camus,* 35.

underpins the ambiguity of Meursault and reinforces the inherently singular ways of responding to the absurdity of the human condition. There is a sense, then, in which *The Stranger* remains profoundly antiphilosophical. Indeed, perhaps this very quality makes for its enduring appeal as a literary work.

SISYPHUS

The Myth of Sisyphus, completed in 1941 and published in 1943, seeks to elaborate a method—if not a system—for confronting a situation in which meaning is withdrawn from the world. It deals with the problem of suicide just as the later treatise of Camus, *The Rebel,* confronts the problem of murder. The "extreme situation" in both books highlights the sanctity of life and the need for a moral stance. The former is the more powerful of the two: it harbors no political pretensions and its topic is directly and emotionally salient.

The suicide rate rises with age, but Camus was aware of the strange attraction suicide has traditionally held for the young since Goethe's *Sorrows of Young Werther.* This older novel of letters is significant here because its main character finally commits suicide over a combination of unrequited love, repressive social mores, and perhaps most important a general sense of weltschmerz. It created an international sensation when it was published in 1775—indeed, Napoleon was said to have read it seven times. The allure of Goethe's work was still apparent in the first decades of the twentieth century, and suicide has remained a dominant literary theme or device. It also remains a prime cause of death for young people, and Camus had himself often contemplated taking his own life.

The Myth of Sisyphus allowed Camus to deal with his own demons. It offers a "lucid invitation to live and create in the very midst of the desert."[13] For this was how he saw the world, as a "desert" in which religion has lost its foundation and science offers no insight into the deep spiritual crisis experienced by the individuals of his generation: "I realize that if through science I can seize phenomena and enumerate them, I cannot, for all that, apprehend the world" (14). Every absolute has been shattered and even philosophy must surrender any systematic claim to "truth." Meaning is lost and a feeling of irremediable despair arises. Life becomes "absurd."

The idea is usually associated with existentialism, which achieved popularity through the writings of Martin Heidegger and Karl Jaspers in the 1920s and 1930s and Jean-Paul Sartre in the 1940s. Individual freedom was the basic concept embraced by all members of this philosophical trend. But they were also concerned with developing some "authentic" way of dealing with death, anxiety, and guilt under circumstances in which an "absolute" such as God is lacking and one ethical orientation is seemingly as legitimate as any other. Camus sought to distance himself from this philosophical movement, and many recent interpretations have essentially supported the supposedly unique character of his stance. Too often, however, they ignore the extent to which the concerns informing his writing reflect those of existentialism.

Camus's way of thinking about the absurd and his other categories, whatever the particular cut he gives them, serves as a case in point. He views the absurd as a particular

13. Albert Camus, *The Myth of Sisyphus and Other Essays,* trans. Justin O'Brien (New York, 1955), v. Subsequent page references to this work appear parenthetically in the text.

encounter between an individual and the world in which the simple habit of living is called into question. It is "that odd state of soul in which the void becomes eloquent, in which the chain of daily gestures is broken, in which the heart vainly seeks the link that will connect it again" (10). Sometimes Camus understands the absurd as an "intellectual malady" and "one perception among many." At other times he characterizes it as defining the limits of our experience and generating an "ontological exigency" for making sense out of the world.[14] Experiencing the absurd is, in any event, neither inevitable nor necessary, and no "right" way of comprehending it is possible. The absurd manifests itself in the "extreme situation," and "lucidity" is necessary for the individual to have "authentically" recognized "the ridiculous character of that habit, the absence of any profound reason for living, the insane character of that daily agitation and the uselessness of suffering" (5).

All of these terms are employed by existentialists, though most give them a unique connotation. Indeed, the interpretation of suicide provided by Camus is fundamentally phenomenological. Camus describes how suicide is simultaneously an expression of and a false response to this experience of the absurd. Suicide militates against both common sense and the visceral experience of reality because it denies that in "man's attachment to life there is something stronger than all the ills in the world. The body's judgment is as good as the mind's, and the body shrinks from annihilation" (6).

Suicide is an act of existential despair deriving from the felt need for an absolute foundation of meaning and the "muteness" of a meaningless world: "That nostalgia for

14. Sprintzen, *Camus,* 46.

unity, that appetite for the absolute illustrates the essential impulse of the human drama. But the fact of that nostalgia's existence does not imply that it is to be immediately satisfied" (13). Suicide capitulates to this "divorce" and allows the absurd to dictate conduct by carrying a logic of meaninglessness to the "bitter end." Since there is no absolute foundation for even this form of logic, however, it becomes illogical and actually carries only an "emotional inclination" to its end.[15] Therein lies its inauthentic quality. Thus, Camus can write:

> In a way, suicide settles the absurd. It engulfs the absurd in the same death. But I know that in order to keep alive, the absurd cannot be settled. It escapes suicide to the extent that it is simultaneously awareness and rejection of death . . . Consciousness and revolt. These rejections are the contrary of renunciation. (40)

There are no external standards. Preserving the absurd without succumbing to it is a matter for the individual alone. The undertaking can proceed in many ways. Intention and experience, however, are always determinative. The "absurd man" can take the form of a lover, an actor, or an adventurer. Essential is only the refusal to hope for eternal life and the willingness to use reason in coming to terms with one's situation. The individual must learn to live without the solace of religion or some prescribed purpose for history or existence. He or she, in short, must learn to "live without appeal" (39).

15. Camus was always suspicious of irrationalism. As a student, he criticized Bergson for giving "some analysis to demonstrate the dangers of analysis, some intelligence to teach one to mistrust the intellect, some fabulation in order to create the idea of fabulation, and, throughout, such oppositions as these." Camus, *Youthful Writings*, 128.

Just as confronting the absurd involves accepting a life without appeal, so must its artistic depiction rest on a willingness to *create* without appeal. "Absurd creation" can offer no didactic lessons and it must resist universal claims. It must treat the encounter with the absurd as a beginning rather than an end. It must explore the "divorce" through which the absurd appears and the resistance it can inspire. Absurd creation must reflect a certain attitude—a sense of "metaphysical honor"—capable of confronting the futility of an absurd existence.

Sisyphus dramatically embodies this attitude. Many legends surround this laborer of the underworld forever condemned by Zeus to roll a huge boulder up a hill, watch it roll back down, and start again. Whether his punishment is for blasphemy, his desire to cheat death, or his love of other human beings at the expense of the gods matters little. He exemplifies the absurd hero.[16] He accomplishes nothing; he receives no reward; he is alone. There is only the moment of consciousness, when he watches the rock roll back down the hill and realizes his refusal of all hope makes him superior to his fate.

> Sisyphus, proletarian of the gods, powerless and rebellious, knows the whole extent of his wretched condition: it is what he thinks of during his descent. The lucidity that was to constitute his torture at the same time crowns his victory . . . The struggle itself toward the heights is enough to fill a man's heart. One must imagine Sisyphus happy. (90–91)

Camus considered his philosophical challenge to the proponents of existentialism as coming down to this: the lack

16. For a thorough if somewhat pedantic criticism of Camus's use of the figure of Sisyphus, see Paul Archambault, *Camus' Hellenic Sources* (Chapel Hill, 1972), 19 ff.

of a predetermined meaning creates the possibility of living life more fully, and this possibility can only become manifest by "keeping the absurd alive" (40). In assuming the importance of remaining alive, however, Camus presupposes precisely what he wishes to defend in his meditation on suicide. His critique rests on circular reasoning, a tautology; only the identification with a particular attitude ultimately justifies his position.

The absurd generates an impulse toward self-destruction, and in response it thus becomes necessary to embrace a certain stance toward life. This commitment is exemplified by Sisyphus. It is undertaken apodictically, or prior to empirical experience and rational argument, thereby allowing for the interpretation of existence in terms of a preexisting personal morality. In framing the argument this way, Camus shows affinities with various existential philosophers and never really progresses beyond J. G. Fichte, the nineteenth-century idealist thinker and forerunner of Hegel, who claimed that the particular inclination of a person will determine his or her choice of philosophical outlook. There is nothing sociological or even psychological about the approach employed in *The Myth of Sisyphus.* The act is stripped of its context: the aged person dying of incurable cancer is left in the same position as the young person contemplating weltschmerz. At the same time, any philosophical or discursive justification is rendered questionable and perhaps even unnecessary. Indeed, there is something dogmatic in claiming that suicide is only rarely "committed through reflection. What sets off the crisis is almost always unverifiable" (3).

But "verifiable" social and psychological problems do tend to make suicide more or less likely. These disappear as the social world disappears.[17] The individual faces the absurd experientially, and the "lucid" appraisal of it, no less than the rebellion against it, shows the same "concreteness," or lack of it, as those existentialists whom Camus opposes and often unjustly accuses of engaging in a negation of reason tantamount to "philosophical suicide." Camus chastises the existentialists for retreating into irrationalism, relying on some notion of the absolute, and entertaining a belief in transcendence. Karl Jaspers and Nikolai Chestov are criticized for their infatuation with revelatory experience, for example, while Edmund Husserl is taken to task for giving intuition a privileged insight into the essence of reality. Søren Kierkegaard and Franz Kafka are similarly seen as retaining the irrational longing for an impossible salvation that, precisely because they understand its impossibility, produces a state of resignation. Nevertheless, just like those he criticizes, Camus is concerned with breaking the stranglehold of rationalist ethics in the name of morality and lived experience.

There is some question whether any of the thinkers dealt with by Camus ever accepted the label or even technically fit under the rubric of existentialism.[18] He emphasizes their belief in transcendence and an "absolute." By way of contrast, or so he claimed, he is willing to rely neither on formal logic nor on experience. He sees his

17. There is something odd about Camus's refusal even to mention the seminal work on suicide, which he surely knew, by the greatest of all French social philosophers: Emile Durkheim, *Suicide,* trans. J. A. Spaulding and G. Simpson (Glencoe, Ill., 1951). The quotation later in the paragraph is from page 31 of this work.

18. Remembering her first meeting with Jean Grenier, Simone de Beauvoir recalled how he asked if she was an "existentialist." Regarding her ideas she was "convinced that they reflected the truth rather than some entrenched doctrinal position." Beauvoir, *The Prime of Life,* 659.

method, which he never really articulates, as standing somewhere between reason and intuition. Its concern is with behavior and what it means to "live *without appeal.*" Camus was indeed confident in the power of absurd creation "to liberate my universe of its phantoms and to people it solely with flesh-and-blood truths whose presence I cannot deny" (75). He wished to claim the "concrete" for himself. But existentialism also sought to present itself as a "concrete philosophy," which is neither "idealist" and metaphysical nor "materialist" and scientistic. Its major representatives were not averse to everyday experience or "self-evident truths"—quite the contrary. Camus wished, however, to carve out his own position. Thus, he maintained that

> knowing whether or not man is free doesn't interest me. I can experience only my own freedom. As to it, I can have no general notions, but merely a few clear insights. The problem of freedom "as such" has no meaning. (41)

Existentialism emphasizes the categorical primacy of "freedom" for a completely valid reason. Unless a person is "free," rather than determined by circumstances or fate, there is no need for him or her to deal with questions concerning the meaning of existence or any possibility of waging a "rebellion" against the absurd in the first place. Even if this were not the case, should freedom or the absurd prove absolute then neither can be seen as an end any more than as a beginning.[19] Belief in an absolute and transcendence is intrinsic to the vision of Karl Jaspers and,

19. Albert Camus, "On Jean-Paul Sartre's *La Nausée,*" in *Lyrical and Critical Essays,* 201.

arguably, Kierkegaard and Chestov. If Husserl believes in either, however, then the meaning of the terms is radically different and Camus himself can be accused of negatively making use of God in his conception of the absurd. Resignation is one possible existential response to the trials of life, but it is never valorized by any of the thinkers with whom he deals.

Neither Heidegger nor Sartre simply relied on formal logic or experience. Both recognized that people must make choices and that the attempt to escape or deny responsibility results in a form of "inauthenticity" (Heidegger) or "bad faith" (Sartre).[20] Such concepts speak to attitudes, which are neither more nor less intuitive and self-referential than those experienced by Sisyphus as he is walking down the hill. Heidegger and Sartre may offer an ontological foundation for existence, which becomes manifest in the unique experience of the individual, but neither offers a belief in transcendence other than in the secular ability of people to question their existence and change the meaning they have previously given it. Indeed, Heidegger and Sartre both explicitly state that neither history nor life has a prescribed meaning apart from the person who lives it or makes it, and that the point is "to give it one."[21]

20. For Camus, *metaphysical hope* rather than *bad faith* is "the continual temptation that ever draws the human being from the possibilities of *authentic* living. Of course, Camus does not talk of 'authenticity' as does Sartre and explicitly seeks to avoid preaching." Sprintzen, *Camus,* 45. But, in fact, *metaphysical hope* is an expression of *bad faith* in Sartre and arguably Heidegger as well. Their categories are as divorced from any prescriptive behavior as the thinking of Camus. It is simply unclear how the concept of "authenticity" is contested. Indeed, certain authors even convincingly suggest that Camus retains it; cf. McBride, *Albert Camus,* 48 ff.

21. Jean-Paul Sartre, "A Reply to Albert Camus," in *Situations,* trans. Benita Eisler (Greenwich, Conn., 1965), 76.

Existentialism is a loose term. It reflects a certain current of European culture as well as a philosophical response to metaphysical idealism and materialism. Camus's
work is part of this current and his thinking part of the
same response to these dominant philosophical trends. It
gives primacy to the "lived life" of the individual; it emphasizes the "meaning-giving act" as did Husserl; it makes
reference to a paradox and the "divorce" within reality
as did Kierkegaard and Kafka; it highlights the "extreme
situation" as did Jaspers; it deals with inauthenticity and
seeks to offer an authentic way of responding to the experiences of anxiety (angst), the absurd, and death; and it is
preoccupied with what Simone de Beauvoir termed "the
solitary man."

The Myth of Sisyphus is an existential work with real
philosophical limitations. But it also expresses a certain
historical reality. It reflects the anguish and the doubts
experienced by the citizens of a defeated France lan-
guishing under the yoke of Hitler. Sisyphus also illuminates the indomitable will of those who survived the
concentration camps in Germany and the Soviet Union.
Camus turned this mythical figure into a symbol of what
is best and courageous about humanity and his tale into
an allegory of the encounter with death and the human
condition. There is a sense in which "Camus felt revolt,
he did not define it."[22] Perhaps for this very reason, the
work gives sanctity to the individual life in a context
wherein many considered it expendable. It treats suicide
as a form of resignation and offers a new existential challenge: the possibility of experiencing happiness without
hope.

22. Todd, *Albert Camus*, 55.

CALIGULA

Camus was still a young man in the 1930s. Whether consciously or not, he recognized the marked difference between his peers and those who grew up in the decades before World War I. Young people all over the world in the 1930s considered democracy impotent, humanism worthless, and individualism decadent. They were drawn to the new movements that demonized such ideals. These movements were led by dictators from both ends of the political spectrum with fantastic ideological plans. Mussolini bragged about building a "New Rome"; Hitler guaranteed an "Aryan" empire that would last a thousand years; Stalin assured his dedicated followers that his purges were necessary in order to bring about a communist utopia. Millions were sacrificed and many millions more suffered war and deprivation for these utopian ends.

A new sensibility emerged during the 1930s. Cruelty took on an almost aesthetic quality as "hardness" became a substitute for pity, "realism" for compassion, "action" for discourse, "resolution" for compromise, elitism for reciprocity. Major writers with markedly differing political viewpoints, such as Bertolt Brecht, Thomas Mann, Ödön von Horváth, Ernst Jünger, André Malraux, Ilya Ehrenberg, and a host of others, noted this new sensibility of the young; it has, again, generally been ignored by most commentators on Camus. Nevertheless, it is crucial for understanding the epoch and works such as *Caligula*.

Camus had initially become interested in the theater just around the time he became active in politics. The Théâtre du Travail, which he founded in 1935, provided him with a sense of community. He changed its name to Théâtre de l'Équipe after his break with the communists.

But the troupe, which included Jeanne-Paul Sicard and Marguerite Dobrenn, stayed together and the program still comprised a mixture of explicitly political as well as classical and avant-garde drama. As the years passed, the founders went their separate ways, but Camus remained fascinated by the theater. He wrote original plays from 1938 to 1949 and adapted various works by important writers from 1953 to 1959. He acted any number of parts during these earlier years and ultimately directed as well. Malraux, who became minister of culture under General Charles de Gaulle, even offered Camus control over the Comédie Française in 1959. Intent on finishing what would become his posthumous novel, *The First Man,* Camus declined.[23]

Camus completed *Caligula* when he was twenty-five, in 1938. The play was based on the portrait of the Roman emperor (12–41 A.D.) drawn by Suetonius (69–140 A.D.),[24] whose writings were introduced to Camus in the lectures of Grenier. The play revolves around the arbitrary exercise of power by this tyrant legendary for his cruelty; surely, everyone was aware of the references and implications when it was first performed in 1945. It shows how each whim of the dictator becomes "necessary" for the realization of his dream. It anticipates the later criticisms of those who would sacrifice concrete individuals in the name of abstract ideals. It exposes the price paid for divorcing means from ends. Above all, it portrays a figure who simply accepts the "absurd" and acts on its implications.

The play is set in ancient Rome after Caligula's ascension to the throne. The young man is initially admired by

23. Quilliot, *The Sea and Prisons,* 45.
24. Suetonius, *The Twelve Caesars,* trans. Robert Graves (New York, 1957), 153 ff.

his court; he is a scheming sycophant, whose words awaken the memory of those conservative elites who thought they could use Hitler and the Nazis for their own ends: "exactly the emperor we wanted; conscientious and inexperienced."[25] Following the death of his beloved sister Drucilla, the emperor is changed. Recognizing mortality, the fact that "men die and they are not happy," he is now filled with scorn and "a desire for the impossible" (8). He experiences the "absurdity" of human existence and, as a consequence, becomes intent on making people live by the light of truth—as he perceives it.

He will now use his power to carry ideas to their logical conclusion. He will place all values on equal footing and thus show the contingent and superfluous character of existence. Guilt and innocence will be rendered irrelevant. The emperor makes it clear to his subjects that "a man needn't have done anything for him to die" (24). Caligula is a revolutionary or, more aptly, an apocalyptic nihilist who wants to change life. He seeks to abolish traditions and everything connected with the past. He blasphemes against the gods, humiliates the patricians, and creates a new order of merit based on the frequency with which people patronize his National Brothel. Consistency disappears as Caligula dispenses favors and punishment. Common sense no longer serves as a guide for living.

> I shall make this age of ours a kingly gift—the gift of equality. And when all is leveled out, when the impossible has come to earth and the moon is in my hands—then perhaps, I shall be transfigured and the

---

25. Albert Camus, *Caligula*, in *Caligula and Three Other Plays*, trans. Stuart Gilbert (New York, 1958), 4. Subsequent page references to this work appear parenthetically in the text.

world renewed; then men will die no more and at last be happy. (17)

Caligula aims to render the impossible possible no matter what the cost. Human life becomes secondary to realizing his dreams of a new world. Caligula wields unlimited power—and he sets no limit on the use of it. All limits collapse: "so long as life is mine, my freedom has no frontier" (14). The absurd is transformed from a metaphysical concept into the condition of reality. Meaning is withdrawn from the world, both in theory and practice. This is precisely what generates revolt not only by remnants of the traditionalist patriciate, but also by Caligula's former friends Scipio and Cherea. The latter puts the matter clearly:

> He's putting his power at the service of a loftier, deadlier passion; and it imperils everything we hold most sacred. True, it's not the first time Rome has seen a man wielding unlimited power; but it's the first time he sets no limit to his use of it, and counts mankind, and the world we know, for nothing. That's what appalls me in Caligula; that's what I want to fight. To lose one's life is no great matter; when the time comes I'll have the courage to lose mine. But what's intolerable is to see one's life being drained of meaning, to be told there's no reason for existing. A man can't live without some reason for living. (21)

Totalitarianism is personified by Caligula, and Camus indicates in the play why he must engage himself against it. He must oppose a situation in which any person can be killed on a whim and wherein "the most preposterous fancy may at any moment become a reality." He detests the arrogance of those who, even with respect to religion, cannot "deny something without feeling called on to besmirch it, or deprive others of the right of believing in it" (43).

Caligula embodies attitudes and values popular during the 1930s: cynicism, arrogance, elitism, and a nihilistic form of utopianism. Such values and behavior, according to Camus, call forth revolt. And not just against Caligula or Hitler, but, in principle, against any dictator, including presumably Stalin. The revolt must even be continual, because, following Saint Augustine, the evil expressed by the Roman emperor is an ineradicable part of the world. This point, which Camus would reiterate in *The Plague,* is made evident when a dying Caligula utters the last line of the play: "I am alive."

Caligula beautifully depicts the experience of those suffering under governments ruling with arbitrary power, and the weakness of the play has nothing to do with Camus's willingness to identify fascism with communism. The political structures of the two systems, if not their ideologies or the socioeconomic circumstances in which they arose, were very similar. Employing Rome as a symbol for the 1930s may make it difficult to grasp the allure different forms of totalitarianism exerted on particular groups or a sense of the divergent social forces leading to its triumph. But everyone got the message. Camus showed the political consequences of an ethical relativism justified by the meaninglessness of life.[26] He also showed the personal decisions and the suffering of real individuals behind what many simply viewed as a totalitarian system—with its own impersonal dynamic fueled by robotic supporters—in which any resistance was impossible.

26. Sprintzen, *Camus,* 77.

The dramatic impact of the play is genuine and the characters are multidimensional. Its problems stem from its central philosophical premise. Camus wished to identify the revolt against Caligula with the refusal to resign oneself to the absurdity of existence. But, in fact, fascism and communism also sought to combat the prevailing sense of meaninglessness and relativism. It is unnecessary to take the absurd seriously as a condition of life in order to revolt against intolerance and the dictatorial use of power. A simple commitment to liberalism, religious values, or even Marxism can motivate political resistance. Thus, if *Caligula* is the first of Camus's works genuinely concerned with the political consequences of the absurd, its metaphysical assumptions are—ironically—unnecessary for illuminating either totalitarianism or the struggle against it.

3 — resistance

Never were we so free as under the German Occupation.
The atrocious circumstances of our fight made us truly live,
without masks and without veils, that unbearable heart-
rending situation called the human condition.

—Jean-Paul Sartre

COMMITMENT

World War II changed Camus. Or, better, it shifted his focus. He experienced something new during this time, in which each, employing a phrase from the play *State of Siege,* "was in the same boat." The earlier concern with the plight of the individual in a meaningless world gave way to a preoccupation with solidarity and the ethics of resistance. The war between Germany and France had seemingly resulted in a stalemate from September 1939 to March 1940. In April 1940, however, the German armies crossed the border, and after a brief period of fighting they entered Paris in June. A sense of betrayal by the old elites, which Jean-Paul Sartre described in *Troubled Sleep,* became palpable. Quickly enough, however, this disillusionment and cynicism were transformed into the militant hope associated with the Resistance.

The Resistance and its aftermath created the context in which Camus became established and joined the circle of Sartre and Simone de Beauvoir.[1] He came to know Arthur

1. An impressionistic and snide account of French intellectuals,

Koestler and Malraux, the poet Michel Leiris, and the brilliant political essayist Raymond Aron. He also fell in love with Maria Casarès, the wonderful actress now best remembered for her supporting role in the classic film *Children of Paradise.* A daughter of the former Spanish prime minister Casarès Quiroga, she worked as a volunteer nurse during the Spanish civil war while still hardly a teenager. She starred in a number of Camus's plays and often threatened to end their stormy affair over his stubborn refusal to leave Francine. Nevertheless, whether as a lover or a friend, Maria Casarès remained his constant companion.[2]

Hers was perhaps the most emotionally charged of the intense relationships Camus forged in the cafés of Saint-Germain-des-Prés, the underground cultural events, the parties at people's homes, and the countless political meetings. Novels like *The Mandarins* by Beauvoir, a roman à clef featuring Camus as a prominent character,[3] would describe how most of these friendships ended after the war. But the bitterness of defeat by the Nazis initially generated a new sense of solidarity, perhaps more intense if just as short-lived, and a hope for the postwar renewal of France from which the legend of the Resistance was born. The postcommunist critique of these French intellectuals, who often foolishly supported the Communist Party, has be-

---

without any real sense of their genuine contributions or the context in which they operated, is offered by Bernard-Henri Lèvy, *Adventures on the Freedom Road: The French Intellectuals in the Twentieth Century,* trans. and ed. Richard Veasey (New York, 1995).

2. Lottman, *Albert Camus,* 316 ff.

3. Simone de Beauvoir, *The Force of Circumstance,* trans. Richard Howard (New York, 1965), 279 ff.

come fashionable and somewhat exaggerated.[4] It is important to recall that "out of the Resistance, directly or indirectly, came nearly every 'advanced' social movement or current of ideas that stirred French opinion from the end of the war until the mid-1950s."[5]

Defeat produced a remarkable response. General Charles de Gaulle fled to London, and, with the help of his supporters, created an antifascist government in exile. Then, following the invasion of the Soviet Union by the Nazis in 1941, resistance groups sprang into existence seemingly everywhere in France. Communists stood in the forefront; their discipline, their hierarchical form of organization, and their commitment drew them many new members. But they were not alone. A cult blossomed around what Sartre would call *engagement*. Even many who were previously apolitical, or former pacifists such as Roger Martin du Gard, author of *Jean Barois* and *The Thibaults* and winner of the Nobel Prize for literature in 1937, found themselves drawn into opposition against Hitler and his puppet rulers of Vichy. A spontaneous solidarity emerged, born of the knowledge that anyone in the Resistance risked imprisonment, deportation, or death at the hands of the Nazis no matter how minor his or her role.

Camus was relatively isolated in the early days following the fall of France. After *Paris Soir* laid him off in order to cut costs in December 1940, he returned to North Africa. He spent the next two years with Francine living a rather frugal existence in Oran, the second city of French Algeria. She took a position as a substitute teacher in an

4. Tony Judt, *Past Imperfect: French Intellectuals, 1944–56* (Berkeley, 1992).

5. H. Stuart Hughes, *The Obstructed Path: French Social Thought in the Years of Desperation, 1930–1960* (New York, 1968), 155.

elementary school while Camus worked as an editorial advisor for Charlot, coached a soccer team, and taught part-time at two schools set up mainly for Jews by the collaborationist Vichy government whose representatives now ruled Algeria. He was too well known to serve a useful role in the Algerian resistance effort. He surely attended various meetings and helped arrange escapes for those wishing to leave Algeria for Morocco or elsewhere. During this time Camus met the antifascist writer and journalist Nicola Chiaromonte, who would become one of his best friends. Basically, however, Camus's existence was relatively uneventful at this time. Then, in August 1942, an attack of tuberculosis led him to convalesce at a sanatorium in Le Panelier, about thirty-five miles south of Lyons, where he began work on *The Plague*.

There he was caught unawares and separated from his wife by the Allied forces landing in North Africa, the first stage of what would culminate in the invasion of Italy in November 1942. Much time passed before he joined the Resistance toward the end of 1943. His hesitancy is somewhat difficult to explain. A National Council of the Resistance (CNR) had already been organized, an antifascist network had existed for some time in the neighboring town of Saint-Étienne, and Jews were regularly smuggled out of France from nearby Le Chambon-sur-Lignon.[6] This town and its heroes surely influenced what would become *The Plague*.

Camus was never a major leader of the Resistance even if he cultivated that image after the war;[7] he had entered

6. Philip Hallie, *Lest Innocent Blood Be Shed: The Story of the Village of Le Chambon and How Goodness Happened There* (New York, 1985), 248 ff.
7. McCarthy, *Camus*, 175 ff.

too late. Once he finally joined, however, he made an exceptional contribution as an anonymous writer and editor of the legendary underground paper *Combat*.[8] Its political stance was explicitly socialist insofar as it advocated a "collectivized economy with political freedom." Its slogan was the same as the name of the well-known Italian antifascist group led by socialist humanists Carlo Rosselli, Carlo Levi, and Ignazio Silone: "justice and liberty."[9]

Combat sent Camus back to Paris during 1943, where he lived first in a hotel and then in the flat of André Gide, which his new publisher, Gallimard, had secured for him along with a modest monthly stipend. Camus did not meet Gide until 1945, but his apartment became a center of intellectual life for the Resistance. Camus quickly made friends with such important figures of the Resistance as Father Bruckberger, who would later greet Charles de Gaulle at the Notre Dame cathedral on his triumphant entry into Paris after liberation; the communist poet François Ponge, who became an intimate friend; and another poet, René Leynaud, chief of the Paris sector of the CNR, whom the Gestapo executed in 1944.

Camus admired Leynaud enormously for his modesty and his bravery. The now famous "Letters to a German

8. "Whenever you asked Camus for a favour, he would do it so readily that you never hesitated to ask for another; and never in vain. Several of our younger friends also wanted to work for *Combat;* he took them all in. Opening the paper in the morning was almost like opening our mail. Towards the end of November [1944], the United States wanted its war effort to be better known in France and invited a dozen reporters to the States. I've never seen Sartre so elated as the day Camus offered him the job of representing *Combat*." Beauvoir, *The Force of Circumstance*, 24.

9. Lev Braun, *Witness of Decline: Albert Camus, Moralist of the Absurd* (Rutherford, 1974), 80.

Friend" were dedicated to his memory.[10] The first of these letters was published in 1943, and the next three in 1944; they became known throughout France. Written as propaganda pieces to justify taking up arms against the Nazis, the arguments are emotional rather than reasoned. Saying that France would emerge from the conflict with "clean hands" or that the Resistance killed without "hating," for example, made sense only in the most polemical terms. For all that, the letters evoke stark images of how a defeated population was forced to live with "silences, with prison sentences, with executions at dawn, with desertions and separations, with daily pangs of hunger, with emaciated children, and, above all, with the humiliation of our human dignity" (6).

"Letters to a German Friend" does not simply justify taking up arms against the Nazis. The letters emphasize the moral cost to the victim of using violence to counter violence. Traces of his former pacifism surface as Camus wonders "if we had the right to kill men, if we were allowed to add to the frightful misery of this world" (6). Questions of this sort he answered in the affirmative. Within the framework of propaganda, however, these letters meditate on the motivations for engagement and reflect the change a generation underwent. They admit the illusions of a time seemingly long past as Camus notes:

> We had to make a long detour, and we are far behind. It is a detour that regard for truth imposes on intelligence, that regard for friendship imposes on the heart. It is a detour that safeguarded justice and

10. Albert Camus, "Letters to a German Friend," in *Resistance, Rebellion, and Death,* trans. Justin O'Brien (New York, 1960), 3–25. Subsequent page references to this work appear parenthetically in the text.

put truth on the side of those who questioned themselves. And, without a doubt, we paid very dearly for
it. (6)

Two traditions are shown in conflict: fascism and humanism, irrationalism and enlightenment, force and what
the French call *civilisation.* These letters made clear for a
general audience the ideological reasons for the war along
with what was culturally at stake. They provide an understanding of what drove young men and women into the
Resistance. They evince the wearying effect of clandestine
meetings, the constant threat of arrest, and the death of so
many friends.

"The three absurds" had revolved around the individual. Even before the first had been completed, however,
Camus began thinking about a second cycle of works with
a new set of concerns. *The Misunderstanding* would serve
as the transition. The purely inner confrontation with the
absurd would now, ever more surely, give way before a different experience of solidarity and a new ethical notion of
social conduct in *The Plague, The Just,* and *The Rebel.*

LANGUAGE

The Misunderstanding was written in the winter of 1942–43,
and it portrays the world of the occupation. The un-
relieved gloom and claustrophobic quality of the play
probably make it easier to read than to see.[11] Perhaps
this helps explain its sharply critical reception when it was
first performed in 1944 with Maria Casarès in the lead

11. Published in tandem with *Caligula, The Misunderstanding* sold
better than any other work by Camus until the appearance of *The
Plague.* Cf. Jürgen Rehbein, *Albert Camus: Vermittlung und Rezeption in
Frankreich* (Heidelberg, 1978), 41 ff.

role.[12] The plot is simple and somewhat contrived. Martha and her mother own a little hotel in a remote valley. They are poor and support themselves by poisoning any rich travelers who happen upon their establishment. One such visitor is Jan, the long-lost son. He has returned from far away with money for his family, but he wishes to be known without giving his name. Maria, his wife, begs Jan to act sensibly and present himself to his family. He remains adamant and sends his wife away, fearing she will betray his identity.

His decision is perhaps understandable as a whim. With the heightening of the dramatic tension, however, it makes ever less sense why Jan should keep his secret. His mother and sister harbor some momentary hesitations about committing yet another murder. But the doubts vanish in the face of habit. Varying the story line of Sophocles' *Oedipus the King*, which deals with a son who unwittingly sleeps with his mother and kills his father, the tragedy of Camus reaches a climax with the murder of the son by his mother and sister. After learning the identity of the victim, the mother commits suicide, and the daughter feels her hopes for a better future have been destroyed. Maria is simply stunned by the news of her husband's death. Martha has no sympathy for her sister-in-law, and following a tense confrontation, Maria cries out for help. But the old manservant, silent until then, answers: "No." With that the curtain falls.

The Misunderstanding was an experiment in what Camus called "the theater of the impossible." But its stilted language and gothic plot undermine this "attempt to create a modern tragedy."[13] Neither critical reflection nor

12. McCarthy, *Camus,* 190 ff.

13. Note the author's preface in Camus, *Caligula and Three Other Plays,* vii.

identification with the one-dimensional characters is made easy. Jan is stubborn. Maria is hapless and weak. The mother is worn down by her existence—she wants this murder to be the last one, and there is a pathetic quality to her suicide following the realization that she has murdered her son. Martha may elicit some sympathy insofar as she desperately wishes to leave her depressing valley for a country by the sea. But she is cruel, selfish, and self-pitying; indeed, even had she known the visitor was her brother, "it would have made no difference."[14]

Tyranny is now seen as infusing everyday life with suspicion and setting people against one another so that, "blind to the commonality of their situation, [the characters] seek to shape the world in the frame set by their essentially solipsistic projects."[15] People turn inward and the sense of community dissolves as the reality sets in that "it's easier to kill what one doesn't know."[16] This highlights the importance of language, which alone makes it possible to establish connections with others. "Silence is fatal," the mother tells her daughter. "But speaking is as dangerous; the little [Jan] said hurried it on."[17]

The Misunderstanding is indeed a play of "missed opportunities."[18] It is now, for Camus, a matter of finding the "appropriate word" in order to identify oneself and intervene in the world. But this is precisely what Jan refuses to do. In keeping silent, he cuts himself off from others and expects intuition to do the work of reason. That is

14. Albert Camus, *The Misunderstanding,* in *Caligula and Three Other Plays,* 123.

15. Sprintzen, *Camus,* 81.

16. Ibid., 79.

17. Camus, *The Misunderstanding,* 123–24.

18. Quilliot, *The Sea and Prisons,* 105.

impossible. Only with language is it possible to deal with a "meaningless" existence and genuinely identify with the sufferings inflicted on the weakest members of society. Thus, the play becomes a tale of "lucidity" betrayed; it makes clear what Camus meant when he once said "one cannot always be a stranger."

SOLIDARITY

The Plague is, arguably, *the* major novel of World War II and surely the greatest novel written about the Resistance. Ironically, it was conceived before the outbreak of the war and written before Camus had committed himself to the Resistance. He was living in the Massif Central, far from the fighting, when he composed the work. Camus felt the war as an absence,[19] which is precisely why he deals neither with battles nor the singular acts of wartime heroism, but the everyday life of a populace under siege. *The Plague* crystallized the experience of a generation sick of war, guilty about its early defeat, and suspicious about the future. It "represents the transition from an attitude of solitary revolt to the recognition of a community whose struggles must be shared. If there is an evolution from *The Stranger* to *The Plague,* it is in the direction of solidarity and participation."[20]

Camus would never again portray as many complex characters with such diverse motivations for action. Written in five parts, reminiscent of the structure used in classical tragedy, this novel has a complex form of narration as well as a subtle mixture of direct and indirect forms of

19. McCarthy, *Camus,* 174 ff.
20. Albert Camus, "Letter to Roland Barthes on *The Plague,*" in *Lyrical and Critical Essays,* 338.

speech. Its sober prose, its careful construction, and its deliberate understatement all contribute to its enduring success. It also provides the best understanding of Camus's political worldview. It most clearly evinces his critique of Christianity, his refusal to love a god who lets the innocent die and who demands unconditional acceptance of the human condition. It reflects the values of the Popular Front, and, like so many other works from the 1930s and 1940s, it has no protagonist. It is a work of great humanism and even greater moral simplicity. There are no grand words and no grand gestures. There is "no question of heroism in all of this. It's a matter of common decency. That's an idea which may make some people smile, but the only means of fighting the plague is—common decency."[21]

The Plague portrays characters driven to political engagement, almost as a last resort, who long for a return to private life. Each retains his own worldview. Each makes choices and, with the exception of a collaborator named Cottard, assumes responsibility for them. Each has, for this reason, a different version of the events initiated by the plague. According to Camus, a "transcendental chronicle" is being presented, which begins with rats dying in the town of Oran, leaving the plague as their legacy, and ends with the subsiding of the disease. People start becoming incurably ill, but the authorities, after first attempting to downplay these developments, cling to habit and refuse to accept the evidence of an epidemic. Thus, ultimately, they find themselves without any plan for dealing with the emergency.

At this point Tarrou unites a motley group of individuals

21. Albert Camus, *The Plague,* trans. Stuart Gilbert (New York, 1948), 150. Subsequent page references to this work appear parenthetically in the text.

into a "sanitation corps" committed to fight the plague. Rieux is a doctor who can no longer heal; Grand is a clerk who wishes to write a novel, but cannot get beyond the first sentence; Rambert is a journalist torn between love for his mistress, whom he wishes to join in another city, and the growing sense of solidarity with the inhabitants of Oran; Paneloux is a priest who, from the pulpit, calls the plague a punishment from God and then witnesses the death of an innocent child; and finally there is Tarrou, a humanist and opponent of the death penalty, who keeps a diary of the plague.

Which of the characters is most "like" the author is an irrelevant question: they all manifest different aspects of the Resistance. Rieux illustrates the militant who, like Camus, doesn't subscribe to any particular political creed and quietly engages in the unheralded day-to-day battle with tyranny; he is "the modern Sisyphus."[22] Tarrou, like Camus, opposes capital punishment and seeks inner peace through his *morale de compréhension*. Joseph Grand, who could never complete his perfect work of art and reflects the writer's block often experienced by Camus, demonstrates his dignity by engaging in the humble task of keeping careful statistics of the plague. Rambert is separated from his lover, just as Camus was separated from Francine, and in staying to fight the plague this character makes perhaps the ultimate personal sacrifice in the name of solidarity.[23] For all his Catholic dogmatism, which Camus experienced while convalescing yet again at a Dominican monastery in 1943, Father Paneloux reflects the courage of his con-

22. Brian Masters, *Camus* (Totowa, N.J., 1974), 64.
23. Brée, *Camus,* 121.

victions. Each of these characters exhibits something with which Camus identifies, and in the solidarity they evince and the sacrifices they make, he finds "more things in men to admire than to despise" (278).

The novel offers no certainty, however, that the struggle against the epidemic is of any use. Resistance does not defeat the plague; it only bears witness against it. The plague seems to subside on its own, and Rieux, who ultimately emerges as the narrator of the novel, ruefully acknowledges to himself

> what those jubilant crowds did not know but could have learned from books: that the plague bacillus never dies or disappears for good; . . . and that perhaps the day would come when, for the bane and enlightening of men, it would rouse up its rats again and send them forth to die in a happy city. (278)

Roland Barthes, the great literary critic, called *The Plague* a "refusal of history." Here is the starting point for any criticism. For this novel of World War II clearly meant "the plague" to stand for the Nazi rulers of France. But numerous critics have noted how the real nature of fascism is ignored and the battle against an inhuman plague oversimplifies the matter of commitment. There is no reason for anyone to identify with a disease. Violence carried out against a human enemy is very different from the tactics undertaken in fighting the plague. Sartre indeed had a point when he noted that the conflicts of interest inherent within a concrete "situation" disappear.

This form of critique is still popular. But it attacks Camus for not having written the "realist" work these critics wanted to read.[24] The critique is external. *The Plague* does not pretend to describe totalitarianism in systematic fashion. The province of a symbolic tale is less the material and instrumental constraints than the moral conflicts experienced by individuals. The book also was not meant to depict the Algerian situation, and it makes little sense to suggest that, from the Arab standpoint, the characters in *The Plague* were not devoted fighters against the plague but the plague itself.[25] Such a seemingly "political" interpretation turns into exactly its opposite: it reflects the kind of ultra-leftism fashionable in the 1960s. The plague symbolically, and the Nazis in fact, would have proven far greater threats to the Arabs than Rieux, Tarrou, or Grand: Trotsky put this type of issue in perspective when, speaking of the battle against Nazi and bourgeois forces in the Weimar Republic, he wrote: when one enemy has a gun, and another a club, first disarm the enemy with the gun.

The Plague was not written about Arab struggle: its political purpose was easily decipherable in the context. This novel was about the Resistance and it stands and falls on its portrayal of this historical experience. Unfortunately, the "realist" political criticism of Barthes and others, such as Sartre, obscures what is historically and politically important about the work. It underestimates the manner in which the novel actually offers a self-understanding of the Resistance. Participants saw themselves, after all, as en-

24. Camus was as little interested in realism as pure formalism. Both were for him symmetrical forms of nihilism. Whether this interpretive stance on the part of Camus actually makes any philosophical or aesthetic sense is, unfortunately, rarely taken into account. But the artist was surely as opposed to merely reproducing the "real" as expelling it in the name of purely aesthetic considerations. Cf. Guérin, *Camus*, 69.

25. O'Brien, *Albert Camus of Europe and Africa*, 55.

gaged in the battle against absolute evil; indeed, men and women of very different creeds united in a common project. Camus glorifies them and perhaps, in a sense, *The Plague* helped foster what would become the "myth" of the Resistance. It offers "an idealised reconstruction of the Resistance movement such as Camus and others would have liked it to have been: the fight of a virtuous and oppressed minority against an anonymous and depersonalized aggressor."[26] But there are also ways in which *The Plague* contests the carefully cultivated postwar image of an overwhelmingly popular antifascism. Its supposed "boyscout mentality" is deceiving. It depicts the majority of the populace as apathetic and falling back into a life of habit as the plague runs its course. Its pessimism concerning the ineradicable character of the plague and its inevitable recurrence, which also obviously brings to mind the fundamental theme in *The Myth of Sisyphus,* undercuts the revolutionary optimism in which France found itself enmeshed following the liberation.

Disease as the symbol of evil and as a basic element of the human condition has a long history, extending from the Bible to the drawings of Albrecht Dürer, the writings of Daniel Defoe and Herman Melville, to the avant-garde dramatic theory of Antonin Artaud.[27] Symbolically identifying totalitarianism with a plague surely obscures the unique character of any political system. Arguably, it even relativizes Nazism in relation to other forms of tyranny. Naturalizing totalitarianism, however, is a double-edged sword. There is nothing xenophobic about the book, which is important given the anti-German sentiment of the

26. Thody, *Albert Camus,* 102.
27. Brée, *Camus,* 116 ff.

time. Evil has no name, no race, no sex, and no nationality. It is part of the human condition. Precisely for this reason, Camus could refuse to identify any one form of evil "in order better to strike at them all . . . *The Plague* can apply to any resistance against tyranny."[28]

Germaine Brée was correct in terming *The Plague* a "cautionary tale."[29] The infectiousness of the disease raises the prospect of contamination, and the doctors are warned about taking the necessary precautions in treating the victims lest they themselves become carriers.[30] In the words of Tarrou, what Camus would consider the basic issue of the age becomes defined:

> As time went on I merely learned that even those who were better than the rest could not keep themselves nowadays from killing or letting others kill, because such is the logic by which they live; and that we can't stir a finger in this world without the risk of bringing death to somebody. (228)

It is not the parable form or the symbolic quality of the tale, but the political values underpinning it that lead Camus to exclude the communists from his narrative. There is not a single communist among the prominent figures in the novel. Rieux, Tarrou, Grand, and Rambert are all liberal humanists; Paneloux is a Catholic and, interestingly enough, a specialist on Saint Augustine. Communists played a prominent role, however, in the Resistance and the common fight against antifascism. Camus's decision to omit them was thus surely purposeful. There is no reason why, from the standpoint of the parable itself,

28. Camus, "Letter to Roland Barthes," 340.
29. Brée, *Camus,* 86 ff.
30. Parker, *Albert Camus,* 113.

he had to ignore the communists or historically distort the Resistance. His decision was based only on what had become a definitive political and ethical position: "There is no objection to the totalitarian attitude other than the religious or moral objection."[31]

Neither Victims nor Executioners, which appeared in 1946, was composed of what were among Camus's last writings for *Combat.* It paid particular attention to the moral element in combating totalitarianism. These essays emphasized the sanctity of individual life and explicitly criticized not only fascism, but Stalinism, for its perverse belief that a utopian future justifies the use of systemic murder in the present. They indeed served to connect *Caligula* with *The Plague.* Their themes were already raised in the former work; in the latter, they become the foundation for a new conception of solidarity. Revolution bows before the attempt to "correct existence" and the desire to articulate what Camus would call "a *rule of conduct in secular life."*[32] Such was the message of *The Plague* when it appeared in 1947.

31. Camus, *Notebooks,* 2: 97.
32. Ibid., 2: 10.

4 — limits

Camus was already a budding star at the time of the liberation. *The Stranger* and *The Myth of Sisyphus* had gained him a following and he was admired as the editor of *Combat*. On his visit to the United States, which he described in his *American Journals,* he was hailed as the most talented of the new French writers.[1] He had also become a father as his wife, Francine, gave birth to twins, Jean and Catherine, in 1945. With the publication of *The Plague,* moreover, Camus conquered poverty. The novel, which soon sold more than one hundred thousand copies and was quickly translated into many languages,[2] turned him into an international celebrity. His lifestyle changed. He briefly returned to Algeria to report on the brutal repression of anti-imperialist demonstrations in Sétif, but he now made the little town of Lourmarin his summer home, kept an apartment on Saint-Germain-des-Prés, and spent the winters in Oran. Camus started wearing expensive

1. Lottman, *Albert Camus,* 376 ff.
2. McCarthy, *Camus,* 231.

suits, drove a black Citroën, and let himself be seen with beautiful women by reporters who followed his movements around the Left Bank of Paris.

Camus enjoyed his fame. But the reasons for his success are not simply reducible to his image as a member of the Resistance or the author of a novel about solidarity. Postwar culture came to be dominated by the existential motifs of *The Stranger* and *The Myth of Sisyphus*. The trials of the Nazi war criminals at Nuremberg and the explosion of new knowledge about the concentration camps created a new preoccupation with personal responsibility and the absurd nature of existence. The extermination of millions generated a concern with the anguish of the individual and the extreme situation in which so many had found themselves. *The Plague* may have reflected the solidarity desired by this postwar world; nevertheless, the novel was already consigned to history before it even appeared.

The Popular Front of the past was dead, and a new version of this progressive coalition never came to fruition. Camus offered no indication of understanding the reasons for its collapse in the past and its lack of feasibility in the present. He sought to preserve the symbolic representation of this organization in his novel without reference to the important role played by communists or the vacillation of liberal humanists. It was the same in the aftermath of World War II when three interconnected issues led to the dissolution of the once vibrant antifascist coalition: the problem of the collaborators, the Communist Party, and the national liberation movement in Algeria. Each would have a profound impact on the career of Albert Camus.

Writing in *Combat* about the collaborators, he initially advocated a policy of "justice without mercy" as the prelude to a radical socialist transformation of French society.

"This country," he claimed, "does not need a Talleyrand, but a Saint-Just." More than ten thousand people died in the purging of suspected collaborators in the immediate aftermath of the liberation by spontaneously organized "popular tribunals." Camus grew increasingly disillusioned with the arbitrary judgments of these tribunals and ultimately he publicly agreed with the earlier criticisms of his position raised by the Catholic novelist and Nobel Prize winner François Mauriac.[3] Camus learned his lesson. He would never again speak in favor of the death penalty and he would remain staunch in his defense of civil liberties.

The constitution for a new Fourth Republic was ratified in 1946. Charles de Gaulle had abandoned his position as head of the provisional government and chose retirement rather than accept what he believed was a state with the same structural weaknesses, the same conditions for disunity caused by a powerful parliament, as the Third Republic. Hopes for a socialist transformation withered as the communists embraced a new sectarian line. Conservatives and remnants of the old right, as well as certain former radicals like Malraux and Pia, now gathered around de Gaulle. Camus annoyed them by calling for an international boycott of Spain, which was under the fascist yoke of Generalíssimo Franco, and by becoming a cofounder in 1948 of the Groupe de Liaison Internationale, which sought to give moral and financial aid to political refugees regardless of ideological orientation. But his opposition to the death penalty and commitment to the politically persecuted also put him directly at odds with the communists

3. Guérin, *Camus,* 43 ff.; Parker, *Albert Camus,* 93 ff.; McCarthy, *Camus,* 213 ff.

who were busily engaged in bloody purges throughout Eastern Europe and, once again, in Russia. Exiles and victims obviously knew about them. They knew also of the concentration camps, the censorship, the constant lying, the egregious policies of the Stalinist regime. But the full horror of the "dictatorship of the proletariat," and its sacrifice of millions for the utopian dreams of an egalitarian society, was not fully grasped. Arthur Koestler, with whom Camus enjoyed a tempestuous friendship, first crystallized this reality for a broader public in *Darkness at Noon.*

Koestler's novel, which appeared in 1940, described a former Bolshevik official coming to terms with his beliefs and previous actions on behalf of the party while facing death in a Stalinist prison. It created a sensation and was instantly condemned by various communists and intellectual sympathizers including, most notably, Maurice Merleau-Ponty. Best known for his work on existential phenomenology and language philosophy, and close to the communists in his younger years, Merleau-Ponty always emphasized the value-laden social context in which the absolute liberty of the individual was mitigated and constrained. His rejoinder to Koestler, *Humanism and Terror,* can be read in many ways: as a hermeneutical inquiry, a reaffirmation of the moment of subjectivity, or a critical endorsement of the Soviet system. In the historical context, it was generally understood as justifying the authoritarian brutality of Stalinism in terms of "historical necessity." Merleau-Ponty viewed the individual as subordinate to the collective and intentions as essentially irrelevant to the social consequences of actions. Thus, even if the "subjective" criticisms made by Koestler were true, Merleau-Ponty thought it necessary to oppose them since they "objectively" weakened the Soviet Union and strengthened its

Western imperialist adversaries in what was obviously turning into a cold war.

Camus was caught in the middle. He supported neither the Western imperialist exploitation of colonies ranging from Algeria to Vietnam nor the brutal policies in Eastern Europe practiced by the Soviet Union. Just after the war, in fact, Camus witnessed the bloody repression of the first Muslim uprising in Algeria against French imperialist rule. His ensuing critical essays were so precise and clear in their demands for the amelioration of conditions in Algeria that he was even offered a government position, but he refused. The army and various conservative groupings were adamant about preserving the imperialist status quo in Algeria. Governmental cabinet after cabinet was paralyzed by the intransigence of the right. The Socialist Party gradually decomposed over the Algerian question and its inability to resolve a mounting set of internal political squabbles and ideological battles. Thus, while the Resistance was fragmenting into communist and Gaullist tendencies, Camus increasingly found himself supporting what Rosselli initially termed a "liberal socialism" whose mass base was vanishing both numerically and institutionally.

Camus refused to make a dogmatic choice between the two sides. His concern about the authoritarian cliques surrounding General de Gaulle caused tensions between himself and Malraux. The communists meanwhile deplored his unwavering commitment to civil rights and republican principles. Camus lauded the Scandinavian form of democratic socialism, but his critics were unsatisfied. They wanted a clear-cut choice between available alternatives in France; they increasingly reminded him that he had never really articulated a political theory or even his fundamental criticisms of the communist worldview and its philosophical foundations. He initially responded with two plays: *State of Siege* (1948) and *The Just* (1949).

State of Siege was conceived as a medieval morality play and a testament less to the general condemnation of dictatorship than to the antifascist struggle in Spain.[4] It shares many conceptual similarities with *Caligula* and, especially, *The Plague.* The action begins with a comet, a bad omen, passing over the walled city of Cádiz. The authorities, intent on maintaining the habits of everyday life, insist that the event did not occur, and therefore should not be discussed by the inhabitants of the town. Preparations for a possible catastrophe are not undertaken, and when The Plague—anthropomorphized as a man in uniform—finally appears, he easily assumes control over the town with the help of a nihilist, Nada, for whom it matters little what government is actually in power.

The Plague, like all dictators, equates the right to power with the fact of power. He introduces a number of arbitrary and noxious decrees that contradict their allegedly beneficial aims. In order to protect the public against infection, for example, he requires each citizen to keep a pad soaked with vinegar in his or her mouth at all times, and in order to prevent contagion, he assumes everyone guilty of carrying the sickness until proven otherwise. The sickness ever more surely isolates people in the community, and the authorities impose ever more drastic measures to end its reign, including executions. This inspires Diego, the hero of the drama, to revolt and The Plague responds with threats against Diego's lover, Victoria. Diego offers to exchange his life for hers, but The Plague refuses and

4. Note the response to the critical review of the play by the Catholic existentialist and politically conservative writer Gabriel Marcel titled "Why Spain?," in Albert Camus, *Resistance, Rebellion, and Death,* 75 ff.

makes a counteroffer: he will end the sickness in exchange for both their lives. Diego is willing to make the sacrifice himself, but he refuses to compromise the innocent. A new form of solidarity is born, and The Plague is ultimately conquered by the common action of the citizenry—even though they realize he can reappear. Thus, for Camus, the moral is clear: immediate political exigencies never justify divorcing means from ends, and no one has the right to choose for another.

The Just more explicitly sets the limits on revolt. French leftists and bohemians traditionally harbored a certain sympathy for anarchism—even if the romantic image of its morally austere and self-sacrificing supporters was always somewhat exaggerated—and its syndicalist variant had proved of some practical importance for the labor movement during the decades prior to World War I. Camus was aware of this and also of how anarchists served as the subjects of significant fictional works such as Turgenev's *Fathers and Sons*, Dostoyevsky's *The Possessed,* and Joseph Conrad's *The Secret Agent. The Just* can legitimately take its place in this tradition.

Written for the legendary French actor Jean-Louis Barrault, based on *Recollections of a Terrorist* by Boris Savinkov, the play is set in prerevolutionary Russia, where the anarchist/terrorist movement was actually quite influential. The play's strong characters, with differing temperaments and ethical views, are all dedicated revolutionaries. The drama revolves around a plot to assassinate a grand duke and deals with issues concerning the moral legitimacy of murder as well as the killing of innocent victims. This becomes evident when Kaliayev goes on his mission, prepares to throw a bomb, and realizes suddenly that the archduke's wife and children will die in the explosion, too. He refuses to act and returns to the group, where a discussion of his decision takes place. Dora, one of Camus's best female characters, stresses that the genuine revolutionary never forgets the empathy with suffering that inspired his or her actions in the first place. Kaliayev then tries again and succeeds in killing the grand duke. He is captured and sentenced to be hanged, but refuses to betray his comrades in exchange for his life. Again the author makes clear that the just society of the future cannot rest on the sacrifice of innocent individuals in the present. Only when a life is exchanged for a life—and even then the actual political value of the action always remains uncertain—is it possible to speak at all about a moral basis for murder. Camus's stance indeed echoed the famous words of Simone Weil: "The moral end is to do nothing which sullies human dignity, in oneself or in another."

While working on *The Myth of Sisyphus,* Camus had already begun collecting notes for a volume concerning the legitimacy of murder. But its completion proved difficult for him. He again suffered from writer's block. He questioned his ability to write a treatise with the requisite philosophical, political, and literary depth. Perhaps Camus even had a presentiment of what would result from its publication. His new work would indeed create a windstorm of controversy, isolate him politically, and cause the breakup of his friendships with Jean-Paul Sartre and Simone de Beauvoir. *The Rebel* would become his first, and last, work of political theory.

REBELLION

The Rebel completed the second cycle of Camus's writings. Published in 1951, it fuses the personal ethic of *The Stranger* and *The Myth of Sisyphus* with the notion of solidarity developed in *The Plague*. Camus hoped this new treatise would place him in the pantheon of the most illustrious French men of letters.[5] It offers a positive response to an absurd existence and simultaneously expresses his revulsion with an age in which mass murder had become accepted as a viable political option. Both concerns are encompassed in the title. *L'Homme révolte* has a double meaning in French: the rebel and the disgusted or revolted man.

The work is divided into three parts, dealing respectively with revolutionary transformation, artistic rebellion, and a political ethics based on "Mediterranean thinking." Its trajectory is clear enough: the political idea of revolution developed by historical thinkers like Marx and Lenin is seen as predicated on certain teleological assumptions about history through which individuals become expendable. This dangerous political perspective is deepened by a form of cultural modernism whose principal exponents, such as the Marquis de Sade, Baudelaire, Nietzsche, and the surrealists, had become intent on abolishing all established social values and customs inherited from the past. In this way, according to Camus, modern revolution is bent on abolishing all limits on action, and for this reason is productive only of nihilism. The third section of the book thus logically calls for reinstating the ethical limits on action, reinvigorating the idea of radical action with a new impetus born of "Mediterranean" moderation, and reasserting the connection between rebellion and compassion for human suffering.

Rebellion is, for Camus, a product of human nature. It

5. Sprintzen, *Camus*, 123.

is the practical expression of outrage at injustice by anyone who has experienced the transgression of a certain limit by a master. The precise definition of this limit is never given; it vacillates between what is established by custom and what is a matter of natural right. But this is not of particular importance to Camus. It is enough that the exploited or oppressed person wants to be treated like anyone else and given respect. Thus, solidarity is implicit in the notion of rebellion, and, in Cartesian fashion, Camus writes the famous line "I rebel, therefore, we exist."[6]

In the revolutionary process, such reciprocity often gets lost. The legitimate goal of countering exploitation is used to justify tactics directly at odds with it (103). The rebel must, using the phrase of Nietzsche, "transvalue values" and contest what is. Rebellion involves transcendence and precisely for this reason, unless limits are placed on it, concrete reality will be sacrificed to abstract teleological notions of History or Reason, with their guarantees of future utopias.

> Rebellion is born of the spectacle of irrationality, confronting an unjust and incomprehensible condition. But its blind impulse is to demand order in the midst of chaos and unity in the very heart of the ephemeral. It cries out, it demands, it insists that the scandal cease and that what has, up to now, been built upon shifting sands should henceforth be founded upon rock. (10)

Attempts to *abolish* the absurd through revolution only reproduce it. All things become possible and all tactics

6. Albert Camus, *The Rebel*, trans. Anthony Bower (New York, 1954), 2. Subsequent page references to this work appear parenthetically in the text.

assume legitimacy, including those involving the murder of any who stand in the way of constructing a just world. The end is seen as justifying the means: abstract claims concerning the need for progress serve to legitimate concrete acts of murder by a movement or a state. Therein lies the "pathology" of totalitarianism. Camus is concerned with the uniquely modern form of mass murder in which no relation exists between the murderer and the victims. Hand to hand combat is out of style and a life is no longer put in jeopardy in the attempt to take the life of another. The possibility of what Camus called "murder by proxy" is precisely what, again, calls for limits on revolutionary action undertaken in the name of liberation. Thus, remembering a conversation with Koestler, Camus wrote in his *Notebooks:*

> The end justifies the means only if the relative order of importance is reasonable—ex: I can send Saint-Exupéry [the famous aviator and author of *The Little Prince*] on a fatal mission to save a regiment. But I cannot deport millions of persons and suppress all liberty for an equivalent quantitative result and compute for three or four generations previously sacrificed.[7]

The rebel must assume that life has an intrinsic worth since, otherwise, he or she would not have contested injustice in the first place. But if this is the case, then commitment to the vision of a perfect world must become tempered by compassion and common sense. The genuine rebel, for this reason, continually strives to remember what motivated his or her undertaking in the face of political

7. Camus, *Notebooks,* 2: 143.

exigencies and the temptation of engaging in unethical action against others. This is precisely what the communist followers of Marx forgot along with those Nazis who perverted Nietzsche's thought.

Building on *The Stranger*, "memory" becomes the enemy of all totalitarians as well as the utopianism through which they legitimate their actions. Their rewriting of history and their arbitrary reconstruction of events are merely derivative. What is really decisive is their attempt to break with *all* of history and thereby elevate an abstract ideal beyond the needs of real individuals. That shatters the connection between means and ends; it necessarily produces an ethical chaos and strengthens the worst and most authoritarian tendencies of the movement. The revolutionary desire to transform the "totality" can only prove disastrous. Thus, Camus wrote: "It's general ideas that hurt the most."[8]

Art supposedly makes this plain insofar as it seeks to create meaning in a meaningless world. Ethical incoherence is denied precisely because art stamps its own form on the real world. But Camus is talking about a particular type of art capable of facing the absurd without surrendering to it. Such an art mirrors the need for rebellion by constantly making reference to the happiness of the individual. It balances form and content. Placing undue emphasis on either is dangerous. For, when art ignores the real conflicts experienced by people, it results in little more than empty formalism. Yet an exclusive preoccupation with *engagement* leads only to dogmatism and monotony. Art must, according to Camus, take a third path between formalism and realism, just as philosophy must

8. Ibid., 1: 27.

reject both pure subjectivism and historical determinism. Indeed, this aesthetic stance mirrors the philosophical position Camus now takes on politics in general.

The symbolic again comes to the forefront. He embraces neither the "no" of withdrawal from public life nor the "yes" of uncritical engagement for one side or another. Camus wishes to stand between the "no" and the "yes." Judgment requires distance and dogmatism must be tempered with the "moderation" born of what Camus calls "Mediterranean thinking." Such notions contest the "passion for divinity" behind all utopian experiments as well as those ambitious plans to transform human nature through which even the best revolutionaries turn into tyrants. They project instead the need for discourse, open-mindedness, and a recognition of human frailty.

Mediterranean thinking considers physical experience, happiness, and creativity as the purposes of every progressive action. It is a way of contesting the absurdity of life. It condemns suicide, by definition, as an inadequate response to the meaninglessness of existence. It also rejects any form of criticism predicated on the ideas that "everything is possible and nothing has any importance" (5). The killing of another person can never prove legitimate unless, in keeping with *The Just,* the killer is prepared to die along with the victim. Denying the possibility for happiness to another through murder, according to Camus, achieves the status of an ethical act only by denying this possibility to oneself through suicide. Both are inauthentic responses to the human condition. But there is a difference between them: murder directly involves the Other. It therefore needs a different kind of definition or understanding. The ultimate social action, murder, demands its limit.

Limits

A willingness to recognize the limits of action differentiates rebellion from revolution. The tyranny of teleology surrenders before a new "principle of reasonable culpability." The validity of the assault on the establishment is now defined by the tolerance extended to others in pursuit of political goals, the willingness to rationally justify claims rather than live in a world of myths, and the ability to embrace positive truths. Indeed, even as a young man, Camus maintained that:

> Politics are made for men, and not men for politics. We do not want to live on fables. In the world of violence and death around us, there is no place for hope. But perhaps there is room for civilization, for real civilization, which puts truth before fables and life before dreams. And this civilization has nothing to do with hope. In it, man lives on his truths.[9]

CRITICISMS

But what are those truths? *The Rebel* begins with the claim that "the first and only evidence that is supplied to me, within the terms of the absurdist experience, is rebellion" (10). And perhaps it is an essential element of the human condition. Rebellion is often, surely, worthy of respect. But since many never engage in such an action, it is difficult to give rebellion the existential primacy of experiences like anguish or hope. There is nothing self-evident about the neo-Cartesian claim that "because I rebel, we exist." It lacks philosophical grounding and it is also highly suspect

9. Albert Camus, "The New Mediterranean Culture" (1937), in *Lyrical and Critical Essays*, 197.

in sociological or political terms. Hegel and Marx argued more plausibly that work provides the initial self-evident experience of intersubjectivity while, in political terms, Camus himself recognized that not every form of rebellion is legitimate. The laudable aim of *The Rebel,* after all, was to put limits on rebellion, differentiate it from revolution, and humanize conflict in the face of the bureaucratic murder of millions by totalitarian regimes.

The Rebel was conceived as a philosophical treatise and as a work of political theory, but there is some question whether it succeeds as either. It is a profoundly humanistic work. Neither its basic assumptions nor its fundamental claims are above reproach and—even at the time—not every criticism was simply ideologically motivated. Not all the criticisms call for an analysis of "the disordered minds to which they attest."[10] The excessive praise of uncritical admirers of Camus as well as anticommunist historians in a postcommunist age is as exaggerated as much of the nasty polemical criticism the work received when it first appeared.

Comparing *The Rebel* with Montesquieu's *The Spirit of the Laws* or Rousseau's *The Social Contract* radically overestimates its importance.[11] It is also clearly not on the same scholarly level as Hannah Arendt's *The Origins of Totalitarianism* or even Erich Fromm's *Escape from Freedom.* Acquaintances of Camus as politically divergent as Victor Serge and Manès Sperber in his magnificent trilogy, *Like a Tear in the Ocean,* also depicted the existential and historical tragedy of communism—along with its ideological allure—far more dramatically. *The Rebel* may have

10. Quilliot, *The Sea and Prisons,* 179.
11. Ibid., 180.

been a product of ten years of historical experience: Spain, the Anschluss, Munich, the war, the Resistance, the postwar purge, the concentration camps. But it was a weary "live and let live" wisdom that Camus derived from these events,[12] and the question remains how well his treatise illuminates them. None of those professing allegiance to *The Rebel* indicates what it actually contributes to our understanding of totalitarianism,[13] revolution, or the importance of civil liberties and republican values.

Camus was surely correct in his critique of teleology and his insistence that the end cannot justify the means because the future will always retain the ineradicable residue of the past. But there is nothing original in Camus's claim that progress starts with revolt or that revolt itself is creative of values.[14] Hegel, Marx, and Nietzsche—each in different and more creative ways—had already argued the same thing. The attempt to connect climate with cultural attitudes, which has obvious racialist dangers, has a tradition reaching back to Montesquieu. The "new impetus" for a reinvigorated politics—moderation—is also as old as *The Politics* of Aristotle. Indeed, whatever the superiority of democratic dialogue to totalitarian monologue,[15] Camus only begs the question: what if the "other" is not willing to listen?

12. Hughes, *The Obstructed Path,* 238.

13. Questionable metaphor substitutes for analysis when Camus writes, "terror and concentration camps are the drastic means used by man to escape solitude . . . Terror is the homage that the malignant recluse finally pays to the brotherhood of man." Camus, *The Rebel,* 247–48.

14. Braun, *Witness of Decline,* 116.

15. "Dialogue on a human level is less costly than the gospel preached by totalitarian regimes in the form of a monologue dictated from the top of an isolated mountain." Camus, *The Rebel,* 283–84.

In its own way, however, *The Rebel* is a visionary work. Its liberal sentiments reflected the burgeoning concerns of the civil rights movement, while its existential preoccupations and commitment to participatory democracy made it seminal for the New Left. It surely anticipated the nonviolent revolutions of 1989 against communist tyranny. Its preoccupation with "dialogue," so popular among contemporary political thinkers, and its belief in reform and the Scandinavian model of socialism are also surely of relevance in the present context. But *The Rebel* was still a work of its time. It illuminated the postwar emphasis by the noncommunist left on solidarity rather than factionalism, humanism rather than determinism, the exploited rather than the proletariat, toleration rather than dogmatism. It stands with other works of the epoch, such as *For All Mankind,* in which Léon Blum demanded a break with the divisive political approach of the left during the Third Republic. It blends liberalism with social democracy and syndicalism, and there are obvious ways in which these three strains in Camus's thought contradict one another. Nevertheless, herein lies its interest.

The Rebel lauds tolerance and compromise. It retains the need for resistance, a "metaphysical" rebellion against the absurd, even as it insists upon the need for moderation, a substitution of rebellion for revolt, in the political arena. Its commitment to parliamentarism and civil liberties is as evident as the author's desire to overcome the inequities caused by the free market. But this is not simply a book for establishment liberals, and Camus is not just another moderate social democrat.[16] He was always suspicious of technocracy, and his book looks back with

16. Guérin, *Camus,* 104 ff. passim.

admiration to the Paris Commune of 1871 and the revolutionary trade union movement, which, "like the Commune, is the negation, to the benefit of reality, of bureaucratic and abstract centralism."[17] Camus was too cynical about the value of sectarianism and too skeptical about revolution to justify any direct identification with the syndicalist political sects of his time. Nevertheless, *The Rebel* stresses spontaneity and—like the great proponents of syndicalism—emphasizes the "point of production," the neighborhood, and the concrete experiences of individuals as sources of rebellion.[18]

Camus liked to say, "I did not learn rebellion in Marx, but in misery." Old forms of revolutionary thinking now lie discarded in the dustbin of history, but the misery remains. Camus's political theory, unfortunately, also has its problems. "Rebellion" and "moderation" are, for example, not quite as compatible in practice as he suggests. The former usually manifests itself in the "extreme situation"; it is supposedly grounded in an absolute notion of reciprocity and human dignity. The latter, if it is anything more than a simple existential attitude, informs politics in the everyday situation and is predicated less on universal interests and ethical norms than on instrumental rationality and material interest. The close connection between pragmatism and reformism is not accidental; reform requires no metaphysical justification other than a belief in compromise and an assumption about the legitimacy of existing institutions.

Intellectuals as diverse as Rosa Luxemburg, Roberto Michels, and Max Weber had already shown how a consistent policy of reform tends to undermine the original moral

17. Ibid., 298.

18. Louis Patsouras, *Jean Grave and the Anarchist Tradition in France* (Atlantic Highlands, N.J., 1995), 102 ff.

impetus of rebellion. The political relationship between rebellion and "moderation" emphasized by Camus is actually, if only for this reason, far more embattled than self-reinforcing. It is questionable whether rebellion can serve as the metaphysical foundation for reform, the primary existential foundation for reciprocity, or the symbol of the human condition. Camus certainly does not argue his case very well. It is also simply insufficient to embrace the initial source of "rebellion" and, *only then,* condemn the alternately perverse or beneficial forms it can take. Enough Nazis and communists joined their movements in order to eradicate or mitigate what they saw as injustice. Many were quite willing to die in exchange for the murder of opponents in brawls and street battles. Each of them undoubtedly also sought to invoke a value and "demonstrate with obstinacy that there is something in him which is 'worthwhile'" (13).

Attempts have also been made by many philosophers and literary critics, such as Ernst Bloch, Harold Rosenberg, Clement Greenberg, and Edmund Wilson, to link Marxism and modernism. Most such attempts are forced: connections are made far more on the level of theory than practice. With Camus, however, the connections and allusions are especially arbitrary: it is comparing apples and oranges, for example, to put Baudelaire and Rimbaud on the same stage with Marx and Lenin. Camus's criticism often loses its focus and there is nothing particularly unique about the approach he employs:[19] numerous other thinkers

19. Camus was content to "discredit the opponent by uncovering his real, partly neurotic motives, and stripping the superstructure under which they masquerade." Especially given the bold manner in which Nietzsche employed this technique, it is a gross exaggeration to claim that this new attempt was "an original and efficient method that Camus applies with great skill." Braun, *Witness of Decline,* 113.

influenced by the idealist tradition used the "critique of ideology" (*Ideologiekritik*) to illuminate the seemingly hidden social or political interests within artistic and philosophical work. Camus's critique, in fact, really amounts to little more than identifying rebellion with those actions of which he approves.

Camus appropriately condemns the manner in which past revolutions generated organs of terror. But he never adequately deals with the constraints in which these revolutionary movements operated or with the inability of liberalism to deal with counterrevolution. He also never makes any reference to institutions, interests, or possible structural imbalances of power in defining "oppression" or "exploitation." He does not even develop the dramatic difference between undertaking rebellion in a democratic as against an authoritarian context. No movement willing to use violence, moreover, can begin with the idea of equally exchanging the lives of its partisans for those of its enemies; it *must* attempt to maximize costs for the enemy and minimize its own losses, and it is simply posturing to speak blithely about the virtues of a stance in which "conscience, if not politics, could be saved."[20]

Most of this got lost in the emotionally and politically charged climate in which discussion of *The Rebel* took place. André Breton, the bohemian leader of the surrealists,[21] reproached Camus for betraying the revolutionary

20. Susan Dunn, "From Burke to Camus: Reconceiving the Revolution," *Salmagundi* 84 (fall 1989): 229.

21. This avant-garde tendency sought to explore the connection between the "real" and what stands beyond it: dreams, fantasy, the occult. For a fuller account, see Marcel Nadeau, *History of Surrealism* (New York, 1992); André Breton, *What Is Surrealism? Selected Writings,* ed. Franklin Rosemont (New York, 1978).

power of fantasy and attacked his symbolic use of the sun as well as his emphasis on "Mediterranean moderation" with the famous statement: "at the center of the most brilliant midday the night is lurking." Humanitarian Catholics, by the same token, were pleased by what some of them considered a "breviary of anticommunism."[22] Communist hacks, unsurprisingly, blasted the book unmercifully, and conservatives applauded Camus for showing how revolutions only produce new hangmen.

Camus had always distrusted the attempts of surrealists to free the unconscious from all social constraints. He surely dismissed the criticism of the communists and deplored the "misunderstanding" of his work by the political right. But even liberal critics, who admired his democratic values and his attack on utopianism, seemed unpersuaded about his philosophical claims such as the absolute value of rebellion. Raymond Aron was snide in complimenting Camus only for being less of a romantic than Jean-Paul Sartre.[23] Thus, there were already legitimate doubts about *The Rebel* before Camus engaged in his bitter debate with Sartre, the dominant figure of French intellectual life in the postwar period.

A CONTROVERSY WITH SARTRE

Camus and Sartre, who was eight years Camus's senior, became friends only during the occupation though each knew of the other's work earlier.[24] Both had grown famous

---

22. Albert Béguin, "Albert Camus, la révolte et le bonheur," *Esprit* (April 1952): 736.

23. Raymond Aron, *The Opium of the Intellectuals,* trans. Terence Kilmartin (London, 1957), 58 ff.

24. Todd, *Albert Camus,* 308 ff., 335 ff. passim.

early in life. But Camus came from Belcourt, a working-class neighborhood in Algiers, while Sartre was part of an upper-middle-class family in Alsace and a cousin of Albert Schweitzer. Camus took his degree at the University of Algiers, while Sartre studied philosophy at the famous École Normale Supérieure. Sartre was short, ugly, talkative, and a man of the city. He despised religion, liberalism, and everything connected with the bourgeoisie. He was, physically and psychologically, almost the mirror opposite of his compatriot.

Camus may have tried to separate himself from existentialism and any other "-ism." His work and that of Sartre, however, initially dealt with similar themes: the individual, the absurd, freedom, and responsibility. Both began as bohemians; both were artists and interested in the theater, both were antifascists, and both ultimately formulated their politics only after the war. Indeed, just when Camus was shifting his focus from individual revolt to the nature of solidarity, Sartre was beginning to incorporate his earlier existential preoccupation with the unconditional character of individual freedom into what would gradually become an innovative understanding of Marxism.[25] They associated with the same circle and, following the liberation, contributed to the intellectual glitter of the Left Bank of Paris.[26]

Much has been written about the relations between these two leading intellectuals of their generation. They competed for a similar audience and they chose different political paths following the fragmentation of the Resis-

25. The transitional work, in this regard, is "Materialism and Revolution" by Jean-Paul Sartre, *Literary and Philosophical Essays*, trans. Annette Michelson (New York, 1955), 198 ff.

26. Beauvoir, *The Prime of Life*, 677 ff.

tance. Each increasingly became more suspicious of the other's ambitions. Camus saw his friend creating an uncritical mystique of the working class, while Sartre saw Camus as justifying Western imperialism in his insistent emphasis upon democracy and the limited character of revolt. The two men had indeed become rivals by 1952. Simone de Beauvoir was surely on the mark when she noted that "if this friendship exploded so violently, it was because for a long time not much of it had remained."[27]

She tells the story of how, in 1946, Camus came to a party and encountered Merleau-Ponty, whom he sharply criticized for his review of Koestler's "The Yogi and the Commissar" and his justification of the terrible Moscow purge trials of the 1930s.[28] Sartre then apparently intervened on the side of Merleau-Ponty, and Camus left in a huff. Sartre caught up with him on the street, and begged him to return. Camus refused. Such was the beginning of their estrangement.

The burgeoning mistrust and misunderstanding between them became public with a review of *The Rebel* by Francis Jeanson in the legendary journal *Modern Times* (*Les Temps Modernes*), founded and edited by Sartre. Camus had apparently asked Sartre to arrange a review, without suggesting any reviewer in particular, and Jeanson volunteered. The result was not what Camus—or Sartre himself, for that matter—expected. Rather than treating *The Rebel* tactfully, as he had originally implied he would, Jeanson attacked Camus for his superficial philosophical interpretations of Hegel and Marx as well as his willingness to

27. Beauvoir, *The Force of Circumstance,* 271.

28. For a somewhat different reading of Merleau-Ponty's understanding of Marxism, see Dick Howard, *The Marxian Legacy* (New York, 1977), 189 ff.

reject revolution without offering any positive or practical content for his vision of rebellion. Camus was furious. Suspecting that Jeanson was merely acting as the front man for Sartre, he wrote a response to "Monsieur l'editeur."[29] Camus essentially dismissed Jeanson, implying he was unworthy of reviewing his book, and attacked Sartre as well as the rest of the editorial board of *Les Temps Modernes* as bourgeois intellectuals and Stalinists unwilling to condemn the concentration camp universe in the Soviet Union.

Sartre answered in a singularly biting and trenchant polemic.[30] He charged Camus with exchanging his earlier nonconformism and commitment to revolt for a fashionable anticommunism. He presented Camus's condemnation of the excesses of both sides in the cold war as a rejection of genuine political "engagement" and an inability to choose between the imperialists and their victims. But there was also a personal attack, and Sartre knew where to push the buttons. He castigated Camus for his arrogant treatment of Jeanson, his sensitivity to criticism, his self-professed weariness with politics, and his moral posturing. Indeed, coming from someone who presumably knew Camus well, all this probably carried greater weight with the public than the political arguments.

Each exaggerated the position of the other. Sartre knew that Camus was not some reactionary anticommunist.[31] For his part, Camus knew that Sartre had steadfastly refused to join the French Communist Party and that he had just recently failed in organizing an alternative movement

29. Albert Camus, "Lettre au directeur des *Temps Modernes*," *Les Temps Modernes* (June 1952): 317 ff.

30. Jean-Paul Sartre, "Reply to Albert Camus," in *Situations,* trans. Benita Eisler (Greenwich, Conn., 1965), 54 ff.

31. Guérin, *Camus,* 105.

of the left called the Rassemblement Démocratique Révolutionnaire (RDR) for which Camus himself had worked
and campaigned. Both were undoubtedly less doctrinaire
than they appeared. How to treat the existence of concentration camps in the Soviet Union, whether they should be
simply condemned or criticized within the political context of the cold war, created a moral divide between the
two men. A *practical* question divided them as well, which
has been consistently ignored. The genuine rather than
the polemical issue was not simply whether to support
the communists or oppose them: it was rather how non-
aligned leftists should act in order to foster a progressive
politics in postwar France where the Communist Party
polled about 20 percent of the vote and received support
from much of the working class, and a democratic socialist alternative had seemingly failed. Each answered the
question differently and herein lay the hidden source of
the conflict between them.

As a revolutionary, Sartre took a "realist" position. He
believed "engagement" within a situation was always necessary and considered progressive politics impossible without the Communist Party. He saw the Soviet Union as, for
better or worse, the only nation willing to identify itself
ideologically with revolution, and, if only for this reason,
Sartre endowed it with a certain "privilege" in the cold
war. It was a strange position for a "realist" to take, given
that the Soviet Union had not pursued a genuinely revolutionary course since 1923. Even while seeking to foster mili-
tancy among the working class, Sartre could never specify
how the Soviet Union or its vassal party in France was actually furthering the revolutionary goal. He was content to
support the Soviet Union insofar as it formally claimed to
represent the working class and the oppressed of the Third

World. His position was abstract from the start. Raymond Aron was surely correct when he wrote that "the philosopher of liberty never managed, or resigned himself, to see communism as it is."[32]

It is not enough simply to juxtapose the warmhearted humanist against the cold-blooded revolutionary intellectual.[33] Sartre and Jeanson, in fact, evinced the same vacillation they criticized in *The Rebel*—they were just a bit more circumspect in expressing it. These fellow travelers stood "simultaneously *against* [the Soviet Union] since we criticize its methods and *for it* because we do not know whether or not authentic revolution is a pure chimera, whether it is necessary in fact for the revolutionary enterprise to follow those paths before being capable of establishing a more humane social order."[34] The difference between them and their opponent really rested on the implications they drew from their theoretical uncertainty. Thus, where Camus exhibited a certain prudence and modesty, Sartre and Jeanson were irresponsibly willing to stake the lives of the masses on a teleological gamble.

None of this has anything to do with a "lack of conviction" on the part of Camus or a refusal to choose sides in the manner of Sartre.[35] Both sought a degree of neutrality in a situation where one was easily labeled a communist or an anticommunist. Each mirrored the doubts and certainties of the other. But where Camus's politics rested on an

32. Raymond Aron, *Memoirs: Fifty Years of Political Reflection*, trans. George Holoch (New York, 1990), 330.

33. Cf. Germaine Brée, *Camus and Sartre: Crisis and Commitment* (New York, 1972), 5 ff.

34. This statement by Jeanson is cited in ibid., 156.

35. Norman Podhoretz, "Camus and His Critics," *The Bloody Crossroads: Where Literature and Politics Meet* (New York, 1986), 47.

absolute rejection of the Soviet Union, coupled with a willingness to place priority on liberal political values,[36] Sartre showed evidence of the general contempt for bourgeois society so noteworthy in his extraordinary autobiography, *The Words,* and a willingness to "privilege" the Soviet Union in its conflict with the West.[37]

Contrary to legend, Sartre was never simply uncritical of the Soviet Union, let alone its brand of Marxism. His journal, *Les Temps Modernes,* actually published an exposé and criticism of the camps in 1947. What he once said of Picasso held true for himself as well: "The U.S.S.R. can neither swallow him down nor vomit him up." Sartre was fearful of having his criticisms of the Soviet Union used to support its opponents. Often he took the side of the Soviet Union explicitly, however, and he logically justified Stalinism when he wrote the ill-conceived *The Communists and the Peace* in the same year as his debate with Camus. But the communists attacked him constantly. They maliciously accused him of collaboration with the Germans,[38] a rumor still current among his critics, and labeled him everything from a "writer of the gutter" to a "pervert." The communists never trusted Sartre and their distrust was justified.

His revolutionary gaze shifted as time passed. He foolishly participated in the communist-sponsored Vienna

36. "The anti-Americanism of Camus, if anti-Americanism there was, remained cultural rather than political and never took frenetic form. The United States occupied a peripheral place in his geography. For him, to repeat, the U.S.S.R. was the principal menace to French democracy, not the [United States]." Guérin, *Camus,* 209.

37. "He felt that its sympathizers should play a role outside the Communist Party similar to that assumed inside other parties by the Opposition: a role that combined support and criticism." Beauvoir, *The Force of Circumstance,* 15 ff.

38. Ibid., 14.

Conference for Peace in 1952, just after the execution of the former Czechoslovakian leaders Slansky and Clementis, and compared its importance with the Popular Front and the French liberation of 1944.[39] But following the workers' uprising in Hungary in 1956, Sartre wrote a devastating critique of the Soviet invasion and its consequences, *The Ghost of Stalin*. He maintained his association with various literary groups dominated by French communists, but his connection with the Soviet Union ever more surely became dictated by its support for uprisings in the Third World and opposition to various Western imperialist adventures, ranging from the Congo to Vietnam.[40]

By 1968 Sartre had identified himself with the strange and anarchistic version of Maoism popular among certain elements of the far left in France. Discontent with one communist experiment only led him to the next. Ever more surely, the "realist" found himself making one unrealistic excuse after another for one Third World "dictatorship of the proletariat" after another. The political judgment of a great intellectual thereby became increasingly compromised, and it has been rendered even more suspect with the collapse of communism.

It was legitimate, and in a way prophetic, for Merleau-Ponty in his *Adventures of the Dialectic* (1955) to castigate Sartre for embracing a form of "ultra-bolshevism." Sartre's vision of the Soviet Union was still clouded by nostalgia for the "heroic years," the period lasting from 1918 to 1923, when it pursued an ill-fated "offensive" strategy in the

39. Todd, *Albert Camus*, 580.

40. For a genuine "realist" analysis of the policies pursued by the Soviet Union in the Third World, which is completely devoid of the illusions Sartre retained, see Richard Lowenthal, *Model or Ally? The Communist Powers and the Developing Countries* (New York, 1977).

international arena and it still had a revolutionary mission to accomplish. His identification with and critique of the Soviet Union were both, from the first, undertaken from an "ultra-left" perspective. As the years passed, his revolutionary Leninism increasingly merged with a type of radical and anti-Western "third-world" populism. But whatever the often narrow political appraisals by otherwise intelligent intellectual historians, and the literary revenge exacted by genuine reactionaries,[41] Sartre was not Ilya Ehrenburg or Roger Garaudy or Eugene Kanapa or Johannes Becher. His major writings remain irreducible to the commitments made by him during the cold war or the Marxism promulgated in either the Soviet Union or China.

The philosophical and literary works for which Sartre remains best known were all written before World War II and his *engagement* with politics. A novel like *Nausea*, plays like *No Exit* and *The Flies*, and philosophical works like *Being and Nothingness* as well as *Existentialism and Humanism* lack any connection with organized politics or political theory. As far as his postwar writings are concerned, with the exception of a disastrous play (*Nekrassov*) and his explicitly polemical works, Sartre never compromised his intellectual independence. His trilogy, *The Roads to Freedom*, remains unfinished precisely because of his indecision about the future of the communist character. His famous play *Dirty Hands* is less an evocation of communist principles than an example of what Simone de Beauvoir called "the ethics of ambiguity"; another of his important dramas, *The Condemned of Altona*, actually contains a self-criticism concerning his role in the debate with Camus.[42]

41. Paul Johnson, *The Intellectuals* (New York, 1988), 125–51.
42. Quilliot, *The Sea and Prisons,* 243.

Sartre's much underrated and unfinished *Critique of Dialectical Reason* was a bold and unorthodox attempt to merge existentialism and Marxism, which the communists condemned as "hopeless idealism." It surely lacked a sustained institutional understanding of the "political,"[43] but its anarchistic strains anticipated the new radicalism of 1968 and justified an assault on any set of institutions identifying themselves with "freedom" or the interests of the working class. Sartre's multivolume study of Flaubert employs Freud in combination with Marxism and existentialism. This work, like his earlier book on Jean Genet, has nothing in common with traditional Marxist forms of biography. It introduces new concepts like the *vecu,* or the nonobjectifiable subjectivity of the subject, which establish his continuing commitment to existentialism. Indeed, until the end of his life Sartre would maintain his affection for Kierkegaard.[44]

None of this is meant to serve as an excuse for the political blindness of Sartre. But the lack of measure with which he has been criticized in the era of postcommunism is as one-sided as the adoration he received from so many during the postwar period. There is a need to restore some perspective in terms of how he should be evaluated. A story told by Malraux is, in this regard, perhaps worth repeating. It seems that during the strike wave of 1968, when Sartre was demonstrating and causing enormous embarrassment for the regime, Malraux suggested jailing him. President de Gaulle supposedly replied: "One does not imprison Voltaire."

43. Howard, *The Marxian Legacy,* 183 ff.
44. Note the superb essay, written in 1964, "Kierkegaard: The Singular Universal," in Jean-Paul Sartre, *Between Existentialism and Marxism,* trans. John Matthews (London, 1974), 141.

Camus was surely right, against Sartre, insofar as the Soviet concentration camps constituted an evil in need of unqualified denunciation, especially since they, necessarily and ineluctably, perverted all the ends that the communists originally sought to realize. Sartre was wrong in claiming that only the "engaged" man has the right to criticize. Such a stance is arbitrary, since no one would make such a claim for fascism, and circular, insofar as the "privilege" implicitly accorded the Soviet Union is itself justified only by belief in an unverifiable teleology. By way of contrast, Camus's emphasis on plausibly connecting means and ends is fundamental for any form of political ethics under circumstances in which teleological assumptions can no longer be taken for granted.

Camus was also more prescient than Sartre in seeing Soviet communism as a moral obstacle for the future of socialism insofar as it suppressed liberty but not injustice.[45] His unwillingness to deal with the communists, however, left him without any political strategy for implementing a democratic agenda. He stood on principle. His was the only French editorial on August 8, 1945, that expressed horror and outrage at the dropping of the atom bomb.[46] He withdrew his support for the United Nations Educational, Scientific, and Cultural Organization (UNESCO) when Franco's Spain became a member, and he protested against the bloody suppression of the 1953 uprising by workers in East Berlin. But he also signed petitions calling for the release of the Rosenbergs, who had been convicted as the Soviet spies they were and sentenced to death in the United States. He opposed terrorism wherever it was employed.

45. Guérin, *Camus*, 112.
46. Todd, *Albert Camus*, 381.

Camus may have tried to walk the "perilous tightrope" between Washington and Moscow, but it is historically inaccurate to claim that, if he stumbled, it was always to the right and never to the left.

Camus took pains to separate himself from the "reactionary bourgeois." There is hardly a single criticism of the Soviet Union made by Camus that could not, and had not, been made by any number of unorthodox Marxists. It is indeed appalling how neoconservatives still demagogically attempt to appropriate his work in the name of anticommunism without any reference to the other philosophical concerns of the treatise.[47]

The Rebel earned Camus many friends among anticommunist anarchists and syndicalists grouped around *Témoins* in Switzerland, for which he allowed his name to be listed as a correspondent, as well as French journals such as *La Libération,* edited by Maurice Joyneux, and the more famous *La Révolution prolétarienne,* edited by Pierre Monatte and Alfred Rosmer.[48] He should also have had some affinity for the small yet intellectually vibrant journal founded by Cornelius Castoriadis and Claude Lefort, *Socialism or Barbarism,*[49] which unequivocally opposed both the Soviet Union and Western imperialism in the name of self-rule of factories by workers or what, in 1968, was called *autogestion.* But Camus kept his distance. Indeed, while his thought harbors certain syndicalist and even councilist elements, Camus never really identified with the utopian and sectarian politics of the ultra-left.

47. Podhoretz, "Camus and His Critics," 33 ff.
48. Lottman, *Albert Camus,* 531–33.
49. Cornelius Castoriadis, "Socialism or Barbarism," *Political and Social Writings,* 3 vols. ed. and trans. David Ames Curtis (Minneapolis, 1988), 1: 76 ff.

Camus actually longed for a genuinely republican front capable of opposing Gaullism as well as communism, and he received approval for such a venture from many in the liberal socialist group around François Bondy and his journal *Les Preuves*. But no mass base for such a project existed in France. Raymond Aron correctly noted that in the postwar era, "as a paper of the Resistance, *Combat* found no place in a regime of parties."[50] That was probably true of the socialist humanism Camus exhibited in *The Rebel*, too. As a consequence, if the "engaged" man appeared as an ideologue, the moralist found himself increasingly isolated.

Sadly, the two great intellectuals of the postwar era were never reconciled. Admirers of Camus and Sartre still argue about who "won" the debate. But there was no winner—only losers. The problem was not that, like so many French intellectuals of the period, they wished to transform society without any understanding of the economic givens.[51] It was rather that, in the final analysis, neither of them was able to connect his principles with a viable idea of practice. The debate between them reflects an epoch in which socialists and communists were irrevocably divided. Both movements had compromised their most radical beliefs and goals in the name of wielding power in a world punctuated by a murderous war just ended, an anti-imperialist struggle under way, and the prospect of a nuclear war always looming on the horizon. Neither the rebel nor the revolutionary could offer a viable theory of engagement or an adequate solution for the most pressing practical political problem of their time—perhaps because there was none available.

50. Aron, *Memoirs*, 156.
51. Ibid., 572.

5 — creation corrected

Camus entered a difficult period after his falling-out with Sartre. The controversy over *The Rebel* actually increased Camus's international standing. But Camus believed Sartre had won the debate, and much of the French public agreed.[1] Even Pia opposed Camus. Pia had come to support de Gaulle and he bitterly resented Camus's decision to shut down *Combat* amid rising deficits in 1947. But he also believed that his former protégé had become too intoxicated with success, too much of a celebrity, and too self-important. Camus was devastated by the avalanche of criticism as well as by the break with Sartre and Pia. His relationship with Francine grew worse: indeed, in *The Fall*, Camus alluded to his wife's attempt to commit suicide. Grand theoretical projects lost their appeal, and, perhaps remembering the success of his last play, *The Just*, he turned to the theater. He adapted a number of literary works for the stage, including William Faulkner's *Requiem for a Nun*, but none of this produced an advance in his

---

1. McCarthy, *Camus*, 254 ff.; Rehbein, *Albert Camus*, 120.

thinking or his art. Thus, feeling stagnant and suffering from writer's block, Camus turned away from France.

In the winter of 1953, he visited the Sahara. Then he went to Holland, Greece, and back to Algeria. It was a time of restlessness and yet another bout with writer's block. But, from his depression and anxiety, he compiled a chiseled little collection of essays entitled *Summer,* which he published in 1954. It begins with the following lines, which reiterate one of the concerns expressed in his debate with Sartre, from "The Minotaur":

> There are no more deserts. There are no more islands. Yet one still feels the need of them. To understand this world, one must sometimes turn away from it; to serve men better, one must briefly hold them at a distance.[2]

The essays of *Summer,* mostly short, reiterate Camus's contempt for any philosophy of history, his suspicions about progress, and his rejection of force as a means of resolving conflicts. He looked to the individual and saw himself getting older. Solidarity makes itself felt again. But rebellion now subtly shifts to the struggle against aging, and, once again, the finality of death:

> In the evening, in the fiercely lit cafés where I sought refuge, I read my age on faces I recognized without knowing their names. All I knew was that these men had been young when I was, and that now they were young no longer.[3]

2. Albert Camus, "The Minotaur, Or Stopping in Oran," in *Summer,* in *Lyrical and Critical Essays,* 109.
3. Albert Camus, "Return to Tipasa," in ibid., 163.

Solidarity cannot compensate for the certainty of impending death or the sense of loss expressed by Camus in his depiction of "towns without a past." But there is also the physical sensuality of "The Sea Close By," which expresses the lure of the Mediterranean and his embrace of a "will to live without refusing anything life offers." Nihilism is still the principal enemy and he holds fast to the Greek notion of "moderation" and the "invincible summer," which he carries in his heart. But, still, more than a hint of bitterness remains. Camus reveals his doubts concerning the ability of an artist to communicate with his public. He criticizes the Parisian intelligentsia, which he likens to piranhas, and their blind desire to identify him with the positions advocated in particular works. Thus he wrote in "The Enigma":

> No man can say what he is. But sometimes he can say what he is not. Everyone wants the man who is still searching to have already reached his conclusions.[4]

Summer had nothing political about it. Ironically, the book appeared during 1954, the year in which the Algerian revolution broke out. No other event would test Camus in the same way. Years of French economic exploitation and racism, lack of political rights for Arabs in Algeria, and religious intolerance for Islam had produced a bloody uprising led by a mass-based National Liberation Front (FLN). As a progressive French Algerian, a *pied-noir,* Camus could not help but identify with this response against oppression. As a French citizen and a humanist, however, he was appalled by the terrorist methods used against Europeans in the course of what would quickly become

4. Albert Camus, "The Enigma," in ibid., 155.

a genuine war. He could take neither side and he condemned those with easy solutions.

Camus gave sustained public support to only one politician in postwar France: Pierre Mendès-France. A hero of the antifascist resistance and an intellectual, an anticommunist and a neutralist in the cold war, a liberal democrat during the 1940s, a leader of the Radical Party and later of the Party of Socialist Unity (PSU) during the 1960s,[5] his liberal minority government of 1954 remained in power less than a year. Before his government fell in 1955, Mendès-France had withdrawn France from Vietnam, started Tunisia on the road to independence, and sought to deal with the Algerian problem. But his policy unfortunately received support from neither the right, which was intent on maintaining the imperial status quo, nor the left, with its insistence on the immediate liquidation of the empire.

Algeria was the jewel in the crown of the French Empire, and even many moderates believed its loss would destroy France as a major power. Mendès-France came under immediate pressure from the followers of Charles de Gaulle, who was spending most of his time in Colombey les Deux Eglises working on his *Memoirs of War,* to put down what began as isolated riots in 1954 and then gradually turned into a mass-based uprising. While holding out offers of economic reform, he sent in French troops to support the governor of Algeria, Jacques Soustelle, who had declared martial law. European sections, mostly white, were gradually sequestered with troops and barbed wire from the native and nonwhite areas. The FLN meanwhile

5. Note the superb biography by Jean Lacouture, *Pierre Mendès-France,* trans. George Holoch (New York, 1984), 211 ff.

gained support in the impoverished, Muslim countryside as it became apparent that the reforms were too little and had come too late. Mendès-France tried to negotiate and offered free elections. His government fell before any attempt was made to realize his promises, however, and a vicious cycle began in which increased repression brought about new acts of terror.

Most intellectuals in France, across the political spectrum, protested the use of torture in Algeria. But lines of division were nonetheless drawn. The far right and most Gaullists were intent on maintaining control of the colony at any price, Sartre and Jeanson sided with the FLN,[6] and Camus associated himself with the policy of Mendès-France. He started writing a biweekly column on Algeria for *L'Express,* a generally progressive magazine owned by Jean-Jacques Servan-Schreiber that supported Mendès-France. In its pages, Camus condemned the violence on both sides. He had only contempt for the imperialist and militarist partisans of the far right. But he also rejected the nationalism and authoritarianism of the FLN. Thus, if he opposed the continuing exploitation of Algeria by France, he also refused to side with those like Sartre and Jeanson who unequivocally supported Algerian independence without regard for the white minority.

In 1956 Camus called for a cease-fire,[7] negotiations leading to free elections, retention of rights by the *pieds-noirs,* the extension of French citizenship to Algerians, and the maintenance of French strategic interests. He opposed

6. Guérin, *Camus,* 163.

7. "In a war in which one side relied on a regular army, while the strength of the other lay in a guerrilla force rooted in the civilian population, such a proposal was so obviously asymmetrical that it could not succeed." Birchall, "The Labourism of Sisyphus," 156.

independence for the colony and instead supported autonomy for it within the French Empire. In his view, national self-determination without republicanism—a Western concept that transcends its Western origins—is always a sham; democracy is the only way in which national self-determination can ever gain genuine and sustained expression. His stance may have been impractical, it may have been idealistic, but it did not simply rest on the thinking of the colonizers.[8] These were still the progressive, federalist, and assimilationist ideas Camus developed in the 1930s when he had actively worked for the Blum-Viollette legislation. But he now seemingly forgot about the successful opposition levied against this policy by the *pieds-noirs*. Even more important, he ignored the new sentiments created by the explosion of national liberation movements everywhere in the colonized world following the close of World War II.

Much has been written about Camus's attitude during the struggle over Algerian independence. Too much of this material deals with the influence on his political position of his "identity" as both a *pied-noir* and someone rooted in Algerian life.[9] The discussion usually revolves around the "authenticity" of his stance and his allusion to the moral difficulties posed by the Algerian conflict in the famous statement made in Sweden after he received the Nobel Prize in 1957:

> I have always condemned terror. I must also condemn
> a terrorism which operates blindly, in the streets of

8. O'Brien, *Albert Camus of Europe and Africa,* 10.
9. Michael Walzer, "Albert Camus' Algerian War," in *The Company of Critics: Social Criticism and Political Commitment in the Twentieth Century* (New York, 1988), 136 ff.

Algiers for example, and which may one day strike my mother or my family. I believe in justice, but I will defend my mother before justice.[10]

Wishing to contest fanaticism on both sides, as usual, Camus posed the matter symbolically. A friend of his mother had been severely wounded during a terrorist action, and Camus sought to draw the consequences. He also knew that under totalitarianism friends had betrayed friends and family members had betrayed other family members. Koestler recounted how the main character of *Darkness at Noon,* Rubashov, handed his comrade and lover over to the secret police, and occurrences of this sort fill Sperber's *Like a Tear in the Ocean.* The philosophical inference is obvious: a belief in limits, in common sense, and basic familial attachments outweighs any commitment to ideology and politics. Only for the worst form of "revolutionary" would the demands of an abstract notion such as justice rule over the real living person: his or her mother.

In fact, the choice was not between Camus's mother and justice.[11] It was between two different perspectives on a concrete situation. Camus confused the issue, and ironically the problem with his position was precisely its symbolic rather than its political character. But he should be taken at his word regarding his opposition to both French colonialism and Algerian nationalism. It is simply not true that "now the humanist in him [gave] way to the *pied-noir.*"[12] It also doesn't help matters to look for his

10. Roger Quilliot, ed., *Camus: Essais* (Paris, 1965), 1881–82.

11. It is certainly not insensitive to note, even for someone who is not a *pied-noir,* that "[t]he statement is finally meaningless. . . . [T]he confrontation of 'mother' and 'justice' seemed to me a clever phrase, not a judgment on a tragic conflict." Aron, *Memoirs,* 255–56.

12. Beauvoir, *The Force of Circumstance,* 362 ff. passim.

estrangement from Arab life in his novels,[13] or emphasize his lack of non-European characters,[14] because Camus was no racist. He was actually a strong public advocate of Algerian writers.[15]

Whether he was rooted in two camps or not as a result of his early experiences in Algeria[16] does not justify his completely impractical politics; it is simply posturing to justify his stance with the claim that his articles were "for all the Algerians,"[17] Arabs and *pieds-noirs*. Indeed, just because he was disgusted with the fanaticism of *both* Algerian national self-determination and French imperialism, his *primary ethical aim* should have led him to embrace the side with the best chance of ending the bloodshed. This was the only concrete position for a humanist ethically opposed to terror to take, and there is a reason Camus himself expressed doubts regarding the viability of his own position.[18]

Realpolitik is not always incompatible with ethical ends; Hans Morgenthau and others could oppose the Vietnam War without supporting the terror of Ho Chi Minh. Given that retaining the status quo was unthinkable, with the *pieds-noirs* opposed to any vestige of compromise, the only practical hope for ending the conflict lay with the FLN. Camus could have said as much. But it was the symbolic

13. Jerry L. Curtis, "Cultural Alienation: A New Look at the Hero of *The Stranger*," *Journal of American Culture* 15, no. 2 (1992): 31–38.

14. Alec G. Hargreaves, "Camus and the Colonial Question in Algeria," *Muslim World* 77, no. 3–4 (2987): 164 ff.

15. Todd, *Albert Camus,* 480.

16. Susan Tarrow, *Exile from the Kingdom: A Political Rereading of Albert Camus* (Tuscaloosa, 1985), 3.

17. Todd, *Albert Camus,* 610.

18. Albert Camus, "Preface to Algerian Reports," in *Resistance, Rebellion, and Death,* 112.

act of standing beyond the extremes, what Vaclav Havel might have termed his "anti-political politics," that ultimately proved decisive. It is indeed simply mistaken to suggest that Camus's various polemical articles and essays on Algeria epitomize what is most valuable in his political thinking—"the idea of a self-limiting, moderate revolt and a principled conviction that political good and evil cannot be simplistically apportioned."[19]

Those general ideas were already elaborated in *The Rebel.* The Algerian situation nearly turned them into platitudes. Emphasizing a plausible connection between theory and practice, or ends and means, cannot occur only on the metaphysical level. Of primary concern should have been bringing the conflict to an end rather than attempting to balance the interests of its participants when compromise had become impossible following the collapse of the government led by Mendès-France. Camus's federalist solution, which took the rights of the *pieds-noirs* into consideration, was compatible with the ethics he had articulated earlier, and it reflected the institutional basis for his internationalist vision. But there was nothing original about his policy proposal. It had no chance of acceptance from either party to the conflict.

His views were "measured," employing a term from *The Rebel,* and they appear enlightened given what would become the authoritarian fate of Algeria with its widespread use of terror by religious opponents of the existing regime. But it is important to remember that the original revolution, whatever the influence of Islam as an anti-Western ideological motivation, was still being fought by a nominally secular movement. Camus's analysis did not delve into the tension between its secular and religious

19. Isaac, *Arendt, Camus, and Modern Rebellion,* 179.

wings. It was not as if he anticipated what was to come. Camus obviously sought to balance his experience of two cultures and two continents, but in fact he transposed the liberal presumption concerning the rational resolution of grievances into a situation in which the institutions for securing such a process were not present. His choice was a refusal to choose between the only serious alternatives available, and, in the context of the time, his vacillations were less than irrelevant: *they actually hindered bringing the conflict to a close.*

Camus approached the Algerian crisis with the good faith of a moralist. But that does not excuse his blindness to incompatible interests, existing constraints, or the basic political issues at stake. Symbolism displaced politics. Camus sought autonomy for Algeria within the confines of the French Empire, but the aims of the FLN were based on the vision of independence. He supported the anti-colonial strivings of the Algerian people, but he refused to recognize the FLN as its legitimate representative. Camus proposed a federal solution beneficial to both French settlers and Algerian natives. Even if the *pieds-noirs* had surrendered their political privileges, such a policy would not only have conflicted with the obvious aspirations for self-rule exhibited by the colonized, but also would have left existing economic imbalances of power intact. The problem was tragically simple: the possibility of dialogue, the keystone of *The Rebel,* was nonexistent. Neither the supporters of the French right nor the Algerian revolutionaries were sustained by democratic or cosmopolitan traditions, and their intransigent attitudes only hardened as the violence grew worse.

Camus found himself politically paralyzed. French and Algerian liberals were invited to Algiers to build a new version of the Popular Front, but he kept his distance since a meeting would necessarily have included the communists.[20] Camus remained adamant in his hope for a noncommunist republican left—a hope that had underpinned his dispute with Sartre. But his appeals for a truce went unheeded[21] and his own proposals ever more surely faded into irrelevance. Camus was left to intervene without much success for various Muslim prisoners condemned to death, and, ultimately, he withdrew from the polemics surrounding the conflict.

The Algerian revolution brought about the downfall of the French Fourth Republic. In 1958, General de Gaulle was asked to form a new Fifth Republic and resolve the crisis. Granted extraordinary presidential power, he turned against his far right-wing supporters and essentially purged the military of reactionary forces. Still, he did not find it possible to grant Algeria its independence until 1962. Neither the right nor the left could have foreseen such a set of developments. The responses of both sides to Camus were therefore entirely predictable. They seemed to agree: the great moralist could not make a concrete political decision.

JUDGMENT

What a gulf between the imagination and the deed!
—André Gide

Issues concerning the character of judgment, interestingly enough, would inform Camus's next literary venture. *The Fall* is perhaps the most beautiful and surely the most enigmatic of all his works. It retains certain religious themes, but it is about more than the fall from grace. It is a

20. McCarthy, *Camus,* 276 ff.
21. Albert Camus, "Appeal for a Civil Truce in Algeria" (1956), in *Resistance, Rebellion, and Death,* 133 ff.

personal work, but it also reflects the climate of the time. It provides a stinging image of Sartre, but it does more than lance the lingering abscess Camus still carried from the debate. It also does not help simply to assert that this novel in which Algeria plays no role is precisely the work in which it is "most painfully present."[22] The value of this novel is even less dependent on its connection with Algeria than on its depiction of the struggle between Camus and Sartre. It rests instead on the questions raised and the possibilities for self-reflection generated. *The Fall* illuminates the costs of vacillation, even as it highlights the dangers of an impenetrable certitude. The novel explores the world of religious atheism in which, like God, authenticity is always sought and always lacking. It resurrects Sisyphus, only this time without any Olympian attributes.

The Fall forms part of a third cycle of works with *Summer* and *Exile and the Kingdom*. In fact, it was originally intended for inclusion in *Exile and the Kingdom*. The short story outgrew its original parameters and it was published as an independent work in 1956. With its cynical tone and underlying satire, its pervasive sense of guilt and opportunities lost, Camus's former concerns with solidarity and a moral code of conduct seem absent from the novel. But that is an illusion. *The Fall*, like *The Stranger*, deals with the existential importance of memory, but with a far greater degree of skepticism given its satirical critique of the omniscient narrator. This novel reveals a world in which memory of the past is inextricably interwoven with lies. The monologue of "a judge-penitent," a derisive term Camus once used to describe the existential-

22. O'Brien, *Albert Camus of Europe and Africa,* 101.

ists, is carefully modified by shifts in setting and various realistic details.[23] But the dramatic success of this *récit,* a form about which Camus learned much from Nietzsche and Gide, depends on the author's ability to make the public identify with the storyteller. The narrator must gradually, if insidiously, draw the public into his monologue. The monologue allows for no contradiction. The reader is gradually turned into an accomplice as the forms of address change from the formal "sir" (*Monsieur*) to the more familiar "my dear" (*mon cher*), to "dear friend" (*cher ami*), and finally to "dear master" (*cher maître*). The reader shares a secret with the narrator supposedly unknown to others. Thus, the tale unfolds. Camus summarized it as follows:

> The man who speaks in *The Fall* delivers himself of a calculated confession. Exiled in Amsterdam in a city of canals and cold light, where he plays the hermit and the prophet, this former attorney waits for willing listeners in a shady bar.
>
> He has a modern heart, which means that he can't stand being judged. Thus, he hastens to try himself but does it so as better to judge others. The mirror into which he looks will finally be held out to others.
>
> Where does the confession begin, where the accusation? Is this a man who speaks in this book putting himself on trial, or his era? Is he a particular case, or the man of the day? There is, in any case, a sole truth in this studied play of mirrors: pain and what it promises.[24]

23. Manfred Pelz, "The Function of the Interior Monologue in 'The Renegade,'" in *Essays on Camus's "Exile and the Kingdom,"* ed. Judith D. Suther (Jackson, Miss., 1981), 190, 192.

24. Cited in Lottman, *Albert Camus,* 564.

Jean-Baptiste Clamence, the main character, is an "empty prophet for shabby times."[25] Once a lawyer and now a resident of Amsterdam, which Camus visited for a few days in 1954, this caricature of Saint John the Baptist lives—like his namesake—in the wilderness, albeit of an urban sort, where he proclaims and satirizes the ideals of solidarity and moral decency on which Camus built his reputation and for which future generations would embrace him. The "Mexico City," a sailors' bar, serves as Clamence's office, where he supposedly devotes himself to the "noble cause" of defending the lowly and the insulted. He even helps blind people cross the street. He has entered this new way of life, left his successful law practice and comfortable bourgeois existence, because he once witnessed a young woman drown herself and found himself either unwilling or unable to help. The recurring memory ultimately produced his "fall" from grace. The satirical play on his namesake is obvious. Indeed, where the real Saint John the Baptist came too early, this one has come too late.

The Fall is another of Camus's parables, and in fact he originally thought about calling it "Judgment" or "The Last Judgment." It is not a realistic novel in which motivations drive the plot;[26] it deals instead with an existential borderline situation, in which the interplay between sincerity and hypocrisy comes to the forefront. Clamence is consumed by guilt, but also by doubt. His culpability is at

25. Albert Camus, *The Fall,* trans. Justin O'Brien (New York, 1956), 117. Subsequent page references to this work appear parenthetically in the text.

26. It is sheer philistinism for a reviewer to consider Clamence "unconvincing" as a character because there is no material reason given why he has thrown away his successful legal practice and comfortable life in exchange for a seedy existence in a tawdry bar. Cf. Podhoretz, "Camus and His Critics," 40–41.

issue, which worries him. In order not to be judged by others, he prosecutes himself, and the irony he employs threatens the values with which the author himself identifies. Clamence is superficially sincere in the tale he tells. But his "authenticity" is really little more than a sophisticated ploy in order to escape the judgment of others.[27] His most nihilistic fantasies are subtly rationalized by identifying them with those of humanity at large. This is what seemingly justifies the abdication of his moral sense and what has been termed his "inner laziness."[28]

Intentions and consequences are again at cross-purposes. Law cannot bridge the divorce between them inherent in an absurd existence. Where dialogue certified the possibility of solidarity in *The Rebel,* and the inner soliloquy evinced the feeling of an honest man in *The Stranger,* the monologue turns into a form of linguistic violence in *The Fall.* The real purpose of Clamence becomes apparent when he says:

> And why should I change, since I have found the happiness that suits me? I have accepted duplicity instead of being upset about it. On the contrary, I have settled into it and found there the comfort I was looking for throughout life. I was wrong, after all, to tell you that the essential was to avoid judgment. The essential is being able to permit oneself anything, even if, from time to time, one has to profess vociferously one's own infamy. (141)

Camus noted in his diary that "according to the Chinese, empires on the verge of collapse have very many

27. Sprintzen, *Camus,* 199.

28. Fernande Bartfeld, "Two Exiles of Camus: Clamence and the Renegade," in *Essays on Camus's "Exile and the Kingdom,"* 288.

laws."[29] The trial becomes less a tragedy than a farce as *The Fall* ultimately reflects a Europe plagued by disillusionment and uncertainty in the aftermath of World War II. The world of Clamence is one of bombed-out cities, uncertainty, and a guilt born of living in a "bourgeois hell." He, like his comrades who suffered through two wars in thirty years, is an "exile without a kingdom."[30] Clamence is a portrait of "all and no one," as the epigraph to the novel, from Lermontov's *A Hero of Our Time,* makes clear: Clamence "is the aggregate of the vices of our whole generation in their fullest expression." The work is not autobiographical,[31] but the moralism and amorous conquests of the character are obviously ironical references to the public persona of his creator, and the satirical references to Sartre are just as evident. Thus, Clamence says:

> I've lost that lucidity to which my friends used to enjoy paying respects. I say "my friends," moreover as a convention. I have no more friends. I have nothing but accomplices. To make up for this, their number has increased; they are the whole human race. And within the human race, you first of all. (73)

Camus surely sought to exert his revenge on Sartre with this novel. What he had lost on the battlefield of philosophy, he now attempted to recover by fighting on a different terrain. He replied through art and, much like his character, by "exposing himself [and] thereby removing himself from the judgment of others."[32] Clamence turns himself into the person who can finally win the approval of the "engaged" individual. He agrees to everything and

---

29. Camus, *Notebooks,* 2: 247.
30. Gaeton Picon, "Exile and the Kingdom," in *Camus,* ed. Brée, 155.
31. Todd, *Albert Camus,* 637 ff.
32. Lottman, *Albert Camus,* 565.

pointedly notes in his musings: "They found me charming, imagine that. Do you know what charm is? A manner of hearing others reply yes when one asks no specific question" (56–57).

Camus simply turns his back on the primacy of the better argument. Sartre used logic against him in the debate and now he has Clamence bow before the victor. Sartre told Camus that he is poor no longer, but rather "bourgeois like me," so Clamence relinquishes all his possessions in order to live with the downtrodden. Sartre condemned Camus for removing himself from the struggle; so, Clamence takes responsibility for everything. Sartre criticized Camus for his moralizing; so, Clamence surrenders morality entirely. His freedom is now absolute, just as Sartre claimed, but Clamence is a bum and also, perhaps in reference to "Saint" Jean Genet—about whom Sartre had written his famous biography—a thief as well.[33] Sartre had attacked Camus for his lack of realism; so, Clamence describes his dream of "being a gangster and of ruling over society by force alone" (54).

But revenge is never all that sweet. Reducing the novel to a critique of Sartre's ontology cheapens it. The tactic of simply refusing to answer the charges against him by ironically agreeing with them, in fact, has more than a hint of dogmatism about it. But most critics ignore this. Instead they choose to see Camus contesting Sartre's world in which isolated egos are engaged in a war of each against all, freedom is "absolute," and the only choice is either to turn the other into an object or to be turned into an object oneself.[34] But, if Sartre considered freedom as absolute in ontological terms, he always embedded it in a concrete context or ontic "situation" wherein constraints exist. In

33. Braun, *Witness of Decline*, 208; Quilliot, *The Sea and Prisons*, 242.
34. Sprintzen, *Camus*, 199 ff., 208 ff.

this context, it is also possible to deal with the other as a subject in his or her own right; indeed, this is what Sartre calls love. Its creation requires less a sense of irony than a willingness to work on building reciprocity within a relationship. Clamence refuses anyone this kind of reciprocity and that choice renders him inauthentic: the character could have been invented, in principle, by Sartre himself.

What was true of *Candide* is also true of *The Fall.* No meaningful critique of a complex philosophical system can be offered in such an indirect literary form. Voltaire set up a straw man when he sought to demolish Leibniz, and it was no different with Camus. Yet, like Voltaire, Camus accomplished something beyond what may well have been his intention. The specific critique of the Sartrean worldview is less important than the willingness to confront a more general concern about the nature of action and the interconnection between authenticity and inauthenticity, sincerity and insincerity, intention and consequence.

Goethe had already raised the issue when he had Mephistopheles say, "it's in destruction that evil is named and that's my authentic [*eigentliches*] element." Nietzsche similarly noted how altruism always hides the will to power. Camus builds on their insights and, whether consciously or not, also those of Sartre. The question then is whether, if authenticity is always intertwined with inauthenticity, these categories retain their validity or the entire concern with moral issues of this sort must instead necessarily devolve into a self-referential "jargon."[35]

---

35. "While the jargon [of authenticity] overflows with the pretense of deep human emotion, it is just as standardized as the world that it officially negates; the reason for this lies partially in its mass success, partly in the fact that it posits its message automatically, through its mere nature." Cf. T. W. Adorno, *The Jargon of Authenticity,* trans. Knut Tarnowski and Frederic Will (London, 1973), 6.

What is true of authenticity, according to Camus, holds also for ethics in general. The critique of authenticity presented in *The Fall*, the inability of its main character to connect intentions with consequences, extends to every notion of ethics as well as the stance of the *moraliste*. Sacrifice is still undertaken and good works are still performed, but "too many people now climb unto the cross merely to be seen from a greater distance, even if they have to trample somewhat on the one who has been there so long" (114). Thus, the novel threatens to undermine the very possibility of developing a coherent ethic capable of informing a moral code of social conduct.

Therein lies the greatness of *The Fall*. It is one of those works in which the artistic imagination, immanently and ruthlessly, calls into question the values held dear by the author himself. *The Rebel* now totters on the reef of insincerity. Absolutes have been undercut and rational dialogue shows its limits. Only an ethical commitment made prior to the engagement or the discourse—what Emmanuel Lévinas, the modern theologian and philosopher, might have termed the "ethic of ethics"—can make a moral outlook possible. A code of conduct can rest only on a pre-rational belief in morality. The absence again defines what is present, and this absence, the hidden longing for faith, is what led many to consider *The Fall* in religious terms and even speculate about the author embracing Christianity.[36]

There is much to justify such an interpretation. There is religious imagery in the book and its basic issues are indeed framed in Christian terms: the thought rather than the act is always what counts. But such imagery and motifs

36. "It is precisely in *The Fall* that numerous pious souls found reasons for announcing the approaching conversion of Camus." Alain Costes, *Albert Camus et la parole manquante* (Paris, 1973), 232.

occur in all of Camus's work. In keeping with the strange dialectic of the novel, which hearkens back to the absurd and the longing for a nonexistent God, Clamence can only seek repentance because he knows it is never forthcoming. *The Fall* does not constitute a break with Camus's earlier conception of the absurd, his concern with solidarity, or even the religious themes of his dissertation. But it trans-figures them. Camus is unwilling to surrender the problem of morality even if dealing with it now must occur in a less categorical or moralizing form than before. The irony of the novel undermines the cynicism its main char-acter extols. No other postwar work, for this reason, prob-ably illuminates quite so clearly the meaning of the fa-mous words by Walter Benjamin: "Only for the sake of the hopeless is hope given to us."

THE KINGDOM

Sisyphus had grown more modest. Camus now joined many of his critics, such as Breton and Sartre, in support-ing the right of French conscientious objectors to refuse active military duty in Algeria. The year 1957 saw the ap-pearance of his "Reflections on the Guillotine," and during this time Camus sought clemency for any number of young Muslims sentenced to death for acts of terrorism. His principal political concern became the contestation of arbitrary power by the state and the defense of *all* indi-viduals condemned for their beliefs. He was strident in his denunciations of the Soviet Union for its suppression of the Hungarian uprising of 1956. Camus made the most of his public presence. But he grew ever more introspective, and the years leading up to his death found him increas-ingly isolated. All his works from this final period express a certain inward turn. Catholic critics, convinced of his impending embrace of Christianity, now squared off against those who insisted he had never questioned his secularism. Both sides probably made it too easy for themselves. Nothing suggests that Camus was ready for a public conversion although he continued to respect what he considered the sacred. This tension unifies the collection of short stories published in 1956 under the title *Exile and the Kingdom.*

The book was not a popular success. It sparked little controversy except perhaps among Catholics such as Mauriac. It also has generally been neglected by critics in comparison with his other works. And basically for good reasons. The writing is often lush, interpretive certainty is undermined, and the stories deal with potentially relevant issues: women's liberation, terrorism, class war, the role of the artist, and the implications of religious faith. It has even been asserted that this collection of stories showed the imagination of Camus coming to grips with Algeria more directly than ever before.[37] But the political or social implications are drawn only in the most indirect fashion, if at all. Each story resolves its conflicts inwardly, outside the political realm, and exhibits longings that inspired the religious atheism of Camus's youth. The period in which *Exile and the Kingdom* and *The Fall* were written is marked less by any overt political self-examination than by a renewed preoccupation with "taking leave of men" and gathering strength in solitude, perhaps, ultimately, "in order to serve them better." This collection of short stories illuminates the incommunicable character of authentic experience: the "other" disappears, since, crucially,

37. O'Brien, *Albert Camus of Europe and Africa,* 80 ff.

what Camus once called "the appropriate word" is never found.

Exile and the Kingdom begins with "The Adulterous Woman," which shows how nature can have spiritual significance. A bourgeois woman of middle age, stifled and unattractive, betrays her conservative husband by surrendering to a pantheistic impulse and experiences an orgasm in the desert night.[38] She feels a new form of freedom as "the whole sky stretched out over her, fallen on her back on the cold earth."[39] But then she returns to her husband and her previous life. She tells him nothing. A feminist message may perhaps lurk in the background, but it fades into a literary expression of "inwardness" (*Innerlichkeit*), whereby an experience is considered transformative without any reference to its effect on the "other." The existential moment is ripped from any context, and the symbolic event turns its back on reality in this story. There is indeed no reason to think that the main character will change her life or even ask herself "profound questions" about its meaning.[40] Her adultery remains metaphysical, and liberation—the exile into the kingdom of nature—momentary and purely subjective. The story is less profound than illustrative of what Hegel once called "the empty depths."

38. The point has been made by O'Brien that in the original draft Camus had Marcel, the husband, make the racist remark, "And people expect them to develop . . . To develop you have to work, and with them work is like pork, forbidden." Dropping this statement from the final version may well have involved less a retreat from issues concerning racism, which receive no sustained treatment anyway, than an attempt to soften the character of Marcel and make the longing of his wife, Janice, that much more personal or existential. Ibid., 81.

39. Albert Camus, "The Adulterous Woman," *Exile and the Kingdom,* trans. Justin O'Brien (New York, 1958), 33.

40. English Showalter Jr., *Exiles and Strangers: A Reading of Camus's Exile and the Kingdom* (Columbus, Ohio: 1984), 27.

"The Renegade," which served as the basis for *The Fall*, employs a far more modernist form and considers exile from the standpoint of religiosity. This second story in *Exile and the Kingdom* takes place during a single day. Built around the soliloquy of a priest, now a slave, whose tongue has been cut out by the fierce tribes of the Taghaza whom he previously sought to proselytize, the dynamic is clear:

> I dreamed of absolute power, the kind that makes people kneel down, that forces the adversary to capitulate, converts him in short, and the blinder, the crueler he is, the more he's sure of himself, mired in his own conviction, the more his consent establishes the royalty of whoever brought about his collapse.[41]

The priest thinks about his conversion to the religion of their cruel and merciless god as he sits in the desert waiting to ambush his successor at the parish. He kills the man. Afterward he cannot help but wonder: "Suppose I am mistaken again!" Doubt undercuts the affirmation of an absolute when the priest stretches out his hand in a plea for redemption; indeed, he cannot help but consider that "death too is cool and its shadow hides no god."[42]

Dogmatic beliefs appear interchangeable: those of the masters and the slaves. The missionary becomes a convert, whose spiritual inability to converse with others genuinely now takes physical form: thrust back upon himself, engaged in an inner dialogue, the former priest becomes his own confessor. He experiences doubt and a moment of authenticity, but there is nothing of Sisyphus in this priest:

41. Albert Camus, "The Renegade," *Exile and the Kingdom,* 39.
42. Ibid., 53.

there is no rebellion against the gods, no moment of lucidity concerning his role in the world, no new understanding of his connection with others. It is enough for him to believe that "there are no righteous men but only evil masters who bring about the reign of relentless truth." The world itself is condemned. The political inference, whatever it is, remains indirect. The priest is left with himself.

Exiled from the kingdom of nature, imprisoned within himself, the existential anguish of the renegade is juxtaposed against the solidarity highlighted in "The Silent Men." This story, which was much appreciated by the syndicalist militants of *La Révolution prolétarienne,* portrays workers in a cooperage factory returning to their jobs after an unsuccessful strike. The industry itself is seen as on the verge of disappearing: shrinking profits for the boss had apparently conflicted with rising living costs for the workers. The boss is no less decent, after his fashion, than the workers. In the aftermath of the strike, however, they take a pledge not to speak to the boss. The workers refuse to reconcile themselves to their situation. Their resentment runs deep, but they are forced to confront it once the employer's child falls ill. The main character, Yvars, wishes to speak: but he finds nothing to say. The need for class solidarity conflicts with the imperatives for human solidarity. Unfortunately, the tension is never played out. Yvars feels pangs of guilt on his way home from work. Sitting with his wife, sipping an anisette, these feelings grow stronger. Ultimately, however, Yvars throttles them. Things remain what they are. Conflicts in which individuals are exiled from one another in society are seemingly incapable of being resolved. There is only the private realm in which the battle of authenticity is fought.

The next story is the most provocative. The inadequacies of silence and the failure to communicate inform "L'Hôte" ("The Guest"). The story concerns a white schoolmaster into whose charge is placed an Arab arrested for murder. Cultures and classes are estranged from one another. The schoolmaster, who cannot speak the language of the Arab, feels a growing sympathy for his prisoner, whom he must take to the village for execution. When they reach a fork in the road, he sets him free. The Arab, however, walks calmly toward the village. He either does what he feels is expected of him or wishes to expiate the crime he apparently committed. The schoolmaster cannot evaluate his decision.

Translated into English as "The Guest," in French *l'hôte* can mean both the guest and the host. The irony is clear: the Arab is a "guest" where he should be the "host" in his own country and the situation is reversed for the schoolmaster. Interesting narrative possibilities present themselves. But, again, the story flounders on the reef of the incommunicable. The two characters are closed to one another. They do not speak the same language either concretely or metaphorically. Even good will is of no use in creating a common ground. Camus had already noted in *The Rebel* that it is "impossible to speak or communicate with a person who has been reduced to servitude," and that servitude itself gives rise to the "most terrible of silences," which "separates the oppressor from the oppressed" (283–84).

Algeria is still weighing heavily on Camus. He maintains his ethical condemnation of violence and terror: the schoolmaster soon enough finds writing on his blackboard stating "you betrayed our brother, you will pay." The unwillingness of the Arab to save his own life puts the teacher under the sentence of death. Perhaps the Arab had planned this, but perhaps not. The teacher is left in the same position as Meursault in *The Stranger:* he, too, is condemned for the wrong reason. Innocent of the crime he supposedly committed, since he liberated the Arab, the schoolteacher is guilty of not fulfilling his prescribed task for the authorities. The irresolvable paradox between intentions and consequences becomes manifest in the story along with the impossibility of communicating the "truth": the teacher is left standing "alone." In this context, however, the ending becomes self-serving: the criteria for rendering an ethical judgment are simply withdrawn by the author. A plague is cast on all houses. The experience of the absurd, contrary to Camus's own aesthetic require-ments, becomes less a beginning than an end unto itself.

Exile and the Kingdom was dedicated to Francine, Camus's wife, who had suffered a nervous breakdown during the summer of 1953. His infidelities and refusal to break definitively with Maria Casarès were apparently among the causes. Camus was grief-stricken and con-cerned about the effect of the disintegrating marriage upon their children. But he needed to seduce even as he felt the need for stability, and this conflict underpins "The Artist at Work." It is the longest story in the collection, and Camus used his personal relationship with Francine as a model. The narrative concerns Jonas, an artist unable to create. Expectation produces writer's block, seductions produce guilt, time is wasted as anxiety increases, and public fame consumes him.

Again, surely in oblique reference to the political criti-cisms directed against him, Camus wrote that "his star de-cidedly protected Jonas, who could thus, without suffering in his conscience, combine the certainties of remembering and the comforts of forgetting."[43] The vacillation of the character is a matter of interest, but nothing is resolved when the story ends. It is not even certain whether Jonas dies or not. There is no connection between the subject and his objectification in works. The artist is apparently not merely exiled from his public and his family, but from life itself, even while he has real work to do and a real public to serve. The ending offers more the posture than the reality of ambiguity when Camus notes how his character printed in the center of his canvas "in very small letters a word that could be made out, but without any certainty as to whether it should be read *solitary* or *solidary*."[44]

Finally, there is "The Growing Stone," the last story in the volume and also the most complex. The setting is the island of Iguape, where the French engineer D'Arrest becomes friendly with Coq, the black cook on a ship, who was saved from drowning when the ship wrecked. Coq considered his rescue a miracle and took a vow that he would carry a heavy stone and lay it at the feet of the Virgin during a religious festival. The reference to the Calvary is obvious, and when D'Arrest picks up the stone after Coq stumbles, the image of Simon carrying the cross for Christ is clear. This story is connected to another in which a statue of Christ floated to shore following a different shipwreck. Every year the citizens take chips from it in a ceremony marking their happiness, and every year the stone regenerates. Making obvious reference to the closing of *The Stranger,* Camus describes the incommunicable and individuating experience of his character as follows:

43. Albert Camus, "The Artist at Work," *Exile and the Kingdom,* 116.
44. Ibid., 158.

And there, straightening up until he was suddenly enormous, drinking in with desperate gulps the familiar smell of poverty and ashes, he felt rising within him a surge of obscure and panting joy that he was powerless to name . . . With eyes closed, he joyfully acclaimed his own strength: he acclaimed, once again, a fresh beginning in life.[45]

It is true: the story's close calls upon the solitary to sit down with his brethren. But the purpose is not merely to eat; it is instead to share with them, silently, their experience of the sacred character of life. Religious metaphors and spiritual forms of solidarity are central, and while the pantheism of the story obviously contests the fundamentals of Christianity, ignoring them in order to depict the worldview of Camus in dogmatically antireligious terms is illegitimate.[46] Nor does it make sense simply to pit the scientific reason of the engineer against the genuinely religious feelings of Coq and others in the village. There is a place for both in the thinking of Camus and a place as well for different forms of spiritual experience, above all the experience of nature. It is perhaps most fruitful to interpret "The Growing Stone" in terms of the attempt of the natural and the sensual to break out of the prison in which modernity has confined them. Playing on the phrase of Max Weber, this story evinces the hope for a "re-enchantment" of the world beyond language and social action.

Such were the concerns of Camus when, in 1957, he was awarded the Nobel Prize. He was among the youngest ever so honored for literature, and, again and again, he

45. Albert Camus, "The Growing Stone," *Exile and the Kingdom,* 212.
46. Brée, *Camus,* 132.

emphasized that he would have voted for Malraux. His acceptance speech was written with lyricism, modesty, and power.[47] He makes reference to other European writers "reduced to silence" and the "prolonged suffering" of his "native land." The speech refers to the struggles of the 1930s and 1940s, and as he rejects all plans to "remake the world," he embraces once again the sensual joys of nature and physical life. Liberal values permeate the address. But, ultimately, it identifies him as an artist rather than a political activist. The writer must assert his independence, and if he provides "a privileged image of our common joys and woes," he must also force himself "to understand instead of judging." Ideology is not his domain: only the "silence of an unknown prisoner subjected to humiliations at the other end of the world is enough to tear the writer from exile." That silence must be articulated and art provides the vehicle; if only for this reason, the artist must keep two commitments: the "refusal to lie about what we know and resistance to oppression."

Camus was undoubtedly thrilled by the Nobel Prize. But what should have been the greatest joy of his literary career, unfortunately, generated new criticisms and bitterness. Mauriac praised him, but *L'Humanité,* the newspaper of the Communist Party, called Camus the "philosopher of abstract freedom," and Pascal Pia, now close to Sartre, sarcastically labeled him a "secular saint in the service of an anachronistic humanism." Parts of the speech tended to inflate his own humility and many surely snickered when he warned against any writer becoming a "preacher of virtue." His symbolic emphasis on the individual and refusal to highlight any particular situations,

47. The address is reprinted in Sprintzen, *Camus,* vii–ix.

where concrete commitments were demanded, offered little by way of response to his critics. Camus's views, according to Pia, perfectly reflected those of a nation like Sweden, which had remained neutral while Norway and Finland were being conquered by the Nazis. Other critics were even less charitable; some even suggested that his award reflected the fact that Camus no longer had anything to say—he had become a classic.[48]

Camus was plunged into a depression. Again he turned to the theater. He produced a new version of Dostoyevsky's *The Possessed* in 1959 and translated Shakespeare's *Timon of Athens*, which deals with a man embraced by his friends for his generosity and then deserted by them in a time of need; indeed, the choice of subject matter reflected his mood. Camus sought an exit. He embarked on new love affairs. Restlessness plagued him. He moved back and forth between Paris and a new house that he bought in Lourmarin, and he traveled to Greece with Maria Casarès.

Nothing worked. Finally, he followed the advice of his last two works: Camus returned to himself.

Perhaps it was in order to make sense of his life, where he was and where he had come from, that he began his last novel, *The First Man,* which remained unpublished until 1994. The precision of the writing is remarkable. The third person provides a voice immediate in its expression of longings and desires yet distant in its cool separation from the events it describes. Here indeed is some insight into the ambiguous word from *Exile and the Kingdom:* solitude and solidarity. The manuscript is a personal memoir of childhood and a search for his father, "a hard man and a bitter one, who had worked all his life, had killed on com-

---

48. Lottman, *Camus,* 600 ff.

mand, had submitted to everything that could not be avoided, but had preserved some part of himself where he allowed no one to trespass."[49]

The art of the book lies in transforming the autobiography of a celebrity into a work of fiction. It begins with the story, told with immediacy and distance, of his own birth. When the tale shifts to Camus the grown man, looking at the tomb of his father, there is the guilt that he has outlived him. His father has grown out of the stone, and again, the image from *Exile and the Kingdom* makes itself felt: the growing stone has become the tombstone with the dates 1885–1914 and the realization that "the man buried under that slab, who had been his father, was younger than he." The son looks at the father like an "unjustly murdered child," and the senselessness of his death in World War I obviously evokes the pacifism so much a hallmark of Camus's later writing. The tale indeed expands from the man to the family left behind, to Camus's beloved mother from whom "nothing was left, neither in her nor in this house, of that man who was consumed in a cosmic fire and of whom there remained only a memory as imperceptible as the ashes of a butterfly wing incinerated in a forest fire" (73).

This indeed is the work in which Algeria emerges. His sympathies are, as he always made clear, with both the Arabs and the *pieds-noirs.* He tells of the founding of French Algeria, the diseases and the terrible hardships undergone by the French pioneers of 1849. The work depicts often awe-inspiring scenes in which lyrical expression

49. Albert Camus, *The First Man,* trans. David Hapgood (New York, 1995), 66. Subsequent page references to this work appear parenthetically in the text.

combines with historical reflection, written by an artist at the height of his powers.

> Ah! Those good people . . . They finished their little shacks in the spring and then they were entitled to cholera . . . They died ten a day. The hot season came early, they were roasting in the huts. And, as for hygiene . . . Later on, they finally gave them land, scattered plots far from the shantytown. Later on, they built the village with earthen walls. But two-thirds of the emigrants were dead, there as everywhere in Algeria, without having laid hands on a spade or a plow. The others remained Parisian in the fields, plowing in top hats, gun on the shoulder, a pipe between their teeth—and only pipes with covers were allowed, never cigarettes, because of fires—and quinine sold in the cafés in Bone and in the canteen in Mondovì as an ordinary drink, to your health, accompanied by their wives in silk dresses. But always the gun and the soldiers around while . . . working in an enemy land that refused to be occupied and took its revenge on whatever it found. (189–90)

Far more than in any other of his works, Camus also brings the victims of colonialism into the picture. The everyday racism they experienced becomes evident throughout the book. The Arabs are a persistent presence in this story about a family of *pieds-noirs*. Their interaction creates the context for the action. Camus describes the ways in which conflicts in Europe spread to the colonialized territories and how both settlers and natives paid the price. Nowhere does this become more apparent than in their thoughts about World War I and "the African troops who melted away under fire like multicolored wax dolls, and each day hundreds of new orphans, Arab and French, awakened in every corner of Algeria, sons and daughters without fathers who would now have to learn to live without guidance and without heritage" (70).

The First Man is a novel of discovery, in which Camus tells of his family and of the world they experienced. It is surely not the upper-middle-class family or the bourgeois world described so trenchantly in Sartre's autobiography, *The Words,* which he published in 1964. Camus makes room for others; Sartre never leaves the stage. Camus is the omnipotent narrator and the stranger; Sartre strips himself bare, chastises himself, and sees the catastrophe of Europe reflected in the intense egoism fostered by his own upbringing. Childhood figures prominently in both works. Camus experiences the sun and the sea; Sartre highlights reading and writing. Camus looks back at the beginning of an unfinished journey; Sartre has already defined himself in his literary tour de force by the age of six. Sartre offers a devastating picture of a comfortable world, ignorant of the imperialism it has already produced and innocent of the fascism it will soon engender, while Camus steps back. There is no blazing indictment. His drama is of a different sort. It is all much less noisy in *The First Man.*

Few novels present poverty with such clarity, such sobriety, such compassion, such anger, and such a lack of bitterness. Camus makes clear what it means to have "grown up in the midst of a poverty naked as death, among things named with common nouns" (60). He mixes insight into the brutality of poverty with the occasional moments of solidarity and honor it generates. The book's classical description almost washes away its filth, but then there are the reminders: the everyday labors, the physical violence, the boredom, the avarice, the illiteracy, the forgetting:

> Poor people's memory is less nourished than that of the rich; it has fewer landmarks in space because they seldom leave the place where they live, and fewer reference points in time throughout lives that are gray and featureless. Of course there is the memory of the heart that they say is the surest kind, but the heart wears out with sorrow and labor, it forgets sooner under the weight of fatigue. Remembrance of things past is just for the rich. For the poor it only marks the faint traces on the path to death. (80)

Camus wished "the book should be heavy with things and flesh" (105), and it is. The novel exhibits almost a tactile quality. There are descriptions of being whipped by his grandmother and of swimming with his friends. The novel speaks of "the curse of work so stupid you could weep and so interminably monotonous that it made the days too long and, at the same time, life too short" (270). It gives a sense of the way in which the child, Camus, grew into an adolescent, and the manner in which early success in school "uprooted him from the warm and innocent world of the poor—a world closed in on itself like an island in the society" (176). There are interesting attempts to untangle his mixed feelings about Algeria and France along with a willingness to experiment with time. There is even a telling note providing a new and intriguing perspective on suicide: "You know my principles. I hate those who commit suicide because of what they do *to others*. If you have to do it, you must disguise it. Out of kindness" (296).

He speaks of his childhood friends, of his mother's loneliness, of the irrelevance of religion, of Louis Germain and Grenier. There are the half-forgotten reminiscences and memories of the past, which would shape his own future. There is the famous story about his father, initially told in "Reflections on the Guillotine," who had applauded the execution of a man condemned for murdering his own family and then became violently sick after witnessing the scene. There are the moments of gentleness like those with Germain where the old teacher states that "at sixty-five every year is a stay of execution," and adds, "I have accomplished nothing," before his former student responds: "there are people who vindicate the world, who help others live just by their presence" (34). There is the realization that in a family dominated by silence no one would inform him about his father: he learns he has "brought himself up alone," informed himself about his father, created his father, and created himself (27, 36).

The First Man was greeted with nearly universal acclaim. Whether that acclaim actually stemmed from the quality of the novel and its recognition of the complexities of Algerian life, residual guilt over the way Camus was criticized during the last years of his life, or the attempt to retrieve him for a "postcommunist" world is an open question. There is a sense in which *The First Man* offered little that was really new. With some exceptions, most notably the reflections on Algeria, the majority of its themes had already been elaborated in his essays: physical pleasure and death, family life and poverty, the sun and the sea, and death. It is still an unedited fragment, and undoubtedly, had Camus lived, the novel would have looked very different. It would have become a work of great breadth and political power. His notes reveal passages intent on describing how "of 600 settlers sent in 1831, 150 died in their tents. Hence the great number of orphanages in Algeria," or of a "lynching scene: 4 Arabs thrown off the Kassour," or a "history of the *Combat* movement," or of "what he wanted most in the world, which was for his mother to read everything that was his life and his being [even if] that was impossible. His love, his only love, would be forever speechless" (286, 294, 296, 300).

As it is, *The First Man* remains a fragment. And perhaps that is only fitting. This autobiographical manuscript was an attempt to preserve the real, the lived life, in art. Therein lies its universality. No life is ever lived to completion, and it is somehow only fitting that this work should have remained incomplete. The draft betrays an ability to sketch a life, highlight a mood, suggest a physical climate, and tell a story. He was not finished as a writer. This last manuscript gives a taste of what might have been and also what was lost when Albert Camus died in a car crash while en route from Lourmarin to Paris on January 4, 1960.

6 — the legacy

The literary public was shocked by the death of Albert Camus. Critics retreated. Obituaries poured in. Exaggerated praise now substituted for the equally exaggerated criticisms of times past. Camus was hailed as a philosophical giant, a political prophet, and a saint. He was even called the "great" writer of *American* literature.[1] Contrary to the fashionable wisdom, Camus was never an "outsider" in the manner of Jean Genet. Camus was a famous man with powerful friends, admired by academic critics as well as a broader public, and his fame carried over in the years following his death.

He was the single most popular writer during the student revolt of the 1960s. This indeed was only logical, given his emphasis on personal responsibility and identification with the oppressed, his pacifism and belief in democracy, his individualism and bohemian sensualism. Only with the collapse of the "movement" would, for a short time, his fortunes change. Camus's work faded from

---

1. Serge Doubrovsky, "Camus in America," in *Camus,* ed. Brée, 17–18.

view during the late 1970s and remained out of vogue for most of the 1980s or what was popularly known as the "me" decade or the "decade of greed." But things changed again with the fall of communism: his advocacy of human rights turned him into a man of the times. His idea of rebellion and his liberal convictions fit the humanistic and constitutional demands of the mass movements in the former Soviet Union and its satellites. But there was a flip side to all of this. His attack on communism was turned into uncritical support for the capitalist state, his individualism was employed against political engagement, and his assault on utopianism became a justification for resignation amid the woes of the world.

Reaffirming the salience of Camus for the next century involves reaffirming the radical quality of his work. It is worthless to extol him for addressing "the deepest mythic level of our being,"[2] and it is insufficient to debate the legacy of his political interventions in terms of whether he was a "just man without justice," or a "good man," or indeed a "noble man."[3] Such talk does Camus no honor. He was no saint; his political judgment was often faulty; and there are many flaws in his political theory. It is necessary to define his legacy more concretely, and perhaps the obituary written by Sartre is the place to begin. Sartre was surely correct when he wrote:

> He represented in this century, and against History, the present heir of that long line of moralists whose works perhaps constitute what is most original in

2. Sprintzen, *Camus*, xiv.

3. Note the genuinely embarrassing discussion in response to Michael Walzer's "Albert Camus' Algerian War" by Lionel Abel, and also Joseph Frank, "Camus and the Algerian War," *Dissent* 32, no. 1 (1985): 105–10.

French letters. His stubborn humanism, narrow and pure, austere and sensual, waged a dubious battle against events of these times. But inversely, through the obstinacy of his refusals, he reaffirmed the existence of moral fact within the heart of our era and against the Machiavellians, against the golden calf of realism.[4]

Camus stands with Sartre in the great intellectual tradition of the moralist, the skeptic, and the activist: Pascal, Montaigne, and Voltaire. A nobility of sentiment informed his political endeavors, a philosophical willingness to engage the larger issues, and an artistic affirmation of solidarity and doubt. Camus reaffirms the tradition of the enlightenment intellectual for our own time. He is concerned with universal problems and he sticks his nose into issues about which he has no expertise. His work fuses politics, philosophy, and art. His characters are lifeless without the ideas inspiring them and his ideas ultimately rest on symbols rather than grounded assumptions: a stone falling down a hill, the blinding sun in the desert, resistance against an ineradicable evil, a monologue in a bar.

Camus speaks to a world bereft of ideological certainties in which any form of "system" is held in disrepute. He wished to distance himself, for better or worse, from all philosophical systems, including existentialism. But, like every other existentialist, Camus sought to break down the wall separating idea and experience or concept and reality. Perhaps he took the enterprise further than the others. He merged the classical form of Europe with the sensual content of the Mediterranean. His craft bathed the world in a fresh light. He depicted the lived moment,

4. Jean-Paul Sartre, "Albert Camus," in *Situations*, 79–80.

and, without surrendering lucidity or common sense, he looked to Greece and North Africa, with their myths, their values of beauty and nature, their notions of balance and proportion, their preoccupation with wisdom and fate.

Totalitarianism, with its sophistic utopianism, coarse fanaticism, and pitiless collectivism, was never an option for Camus. It was easy for him to take sides in the battles between democracies and dictatorships. Choice became more difficult when the imperialism undertaken by democratic states came into conflict with authoritarian movements for national liberation. The moralist vacillated in these situations. Camus came under attack by the Left and the Right. He had as little use for imperialism as for nationalism. He attempted to counter both with calls for tolerance and democracy. He refused to bend his principles in response to the exigencies of political practice, and his approach was probably counterproductive in the historical context of Algeria. He was not a political prophet: he never genuinely considered questions concerning the fragility of what would become an Algerian republic, the potential for dictatorship, the issue of religious fanaticism, or the likelihood of what would become a virtual civil war between secularists and believers. He simply and consistently opposed terror. The issue for him was the tactic rather than the political culture in which it was embedded.

But Camus anticipated a new historical constellation. His commitment to principle and his ability to see both sides of an issue provide a telling example for a multilateral world in which the old ideological certainties have vanished. There is even a lesson in his vacillations. He implicitly recognized the difference between politicians and intellectuals: the former must choose with respect to the possible while the latter have the luxury to withhold support from one side or another in the name of those values through which the emancipatory struggle gains its purpose. Camus makes it clear that the intellectual must retain the right, as well as the liberty, to express his or her feelings of uncertainty. In this vein, he always refused the role of a cultural propagandist, and he hated the gesture of radicalism. This is the sense in which Camus could say, "I prefer committed men to literatures of commitment."[5]

The symbol of justice, for him, always jutted beyond the complex of interests and institutions with which it was enmeshed. Camus could, for this reason, identify with the individual beyond all points of dogma. He was never tempted by absolute claims or self-serving justifications for terrorist policies, and for him national self-determination without republicanism was meaningless. The world is still largely ruled by authoritarian regimes and there is nothing trite about the emphasis Camus placed on constitutions and civil liberties. He was among those who recognized that these institutions alone protect the individual from the exercise of arbitrary power and enable him or her to deal with their private fate. Nelson Mandela and Weng Jingsheng, who spent many years in the prisons of Chinese communism, exemplify contemporary figures with whom Camus would have identified. He prized honesty and the moment in which an individual recognizes his or her responsibility and solidarity with others. But he also understood that politics and political participation are not necessarily primary or an end unto themselves. Rather, these should create the preconditions for more personal forms of exploration and enjoyment. Camus was among the very few thinkers of his generation who put a philosophical

5. Camus, *Notebooks,* 2: 140.

premium on happiness. Perhaps because he had tuberculosis, he never turned death into a fetish as Heidegger did, and, surely because he once knew real poverty, he never idealized the poor as Sartre did.

Camus generalized from his own impressions and used his art to provide them with a universal stamp. The main characters in his novels would probably have liked one another. Sisyphus, Meursault, Rieux, and the rest all exhibit a mixture of skepticism and tolerance, lucidity and courage, a sense of responsibility and a willingness to learn. Even Clamence had his moments. Camus might well have been speaking of himself when he wrote that "a man's work is nothing but this slow trek to rediscover, through the detours of art, those two or three great and simple images in whose presence his heart first opened."[6] The novel was for him nothing more than philosophy put in images; he wrote of Sartre's *Nausea* that "in a good novel all the philosophy is passed along through the images." The insight pertains to his own work as well. He was less successful when he tried to present his ideas in a systematic fashion—and he knew it. "I am not a philosopher, and I know how to speak only of what I experienced."[7]

There were costs for his philosophical inadequacies.[8] The concepts he valorized, such as solidarity and resistance, were defined so vaguely that they could be embraced by

6. Camus, "Preface of 1958" to *The Wrong Side and the Right Side,* 17.

7. Cited in Serge Doubrovsky, "The Ethics of Albert Camus," in *Camus,* ed. Brée, 72.

8. It is both anti-intellectual and simply foolish to claim that "because he was not a philosopher but a simple man endowed with the genius of expression, Camus is close to all of us and is all the more engaging a witness by virtue of his not being excessively gifted in the use of dialectics and the spirit of synthesis." Onimus, *Albert Camus and Christianity,* 3; also Sprintzen, *Camus,* 121; Brée, *Camus,* 8 passim.

anyone and were so obvious in their appeal that criticism was virtually impossible. The lack of any systematic articulation rendered his thinking arbitrary, undermined any coherent connection between theory and practice, and sometimes threatened the lucidity he prized. Fortunately, he never turned experience into the criterion of truth. He saw the danger of irrationalism, the forms uncritical belief can take, and the way it can turn into fanaticism. Camus put a premium on doubt when he wrote: "The militant too quickly convinced is to the true revolutionary what the bigot is to a mystic. The grandeur of a faith can be measured by the doubts it inspires."[9]

Themes of a religious sort surely inspired him from the beginning. The titles of his last books, *The Fall* and *Exile and the Kingdom,* speak for themselves and the absurd is ultimately defined by a religious longing even if it is predicated on the absence of God. Whatever his spiritual inclinations, however, the dogma of organized religion appealed to him as little as what became the catechism of Marxism. The absurd, the meaninglessness of existence, is the reality with which each individual has to deal. The foundation of the individual is freedom: the choice made with respect to the absurd. For Camus, in contrast to other existentialists, recognizing the absurd is only the beginning. The question is whether the individual will also contest its implications: first with courage and lucidity, then with solidarity.[10] Therein lies Camus's rebellion against the deduction made famous by one of Dostoyevsky's characters: "If God does not exist then everything is permitted."

9. Albert Camus, "Review of *Bread and Wine* by Ignazio Silone," in *Lyrical and Critical Essays,* 208.

10. François Bousquet, *Camus le Méditerranéen Camus l'Ancien* (Quebec, 1977), 104.

The rebel is not a revolutionary. His actions show limits. Without limits, Camus feared, action will be preserved from ethical claims and it will take on an inhuman dynamic. The denial of limits thrusts action into the abyss and buttresses the absurd, whatever the sacrifices undertaken in the name of abolishing it. Action without limits underpins the violence exercised by any totalitarian movement or regime; it justifies the exercise of arbitrary power. Power of this sort, which relies on coercion rather than persuasion, was precisely what Camus wished to curtail when he wrote: "We must serve justice because our condition is unjust, increase happiness and joy because this universe is unhappy. Likewise, we must not condemn others to death because we have been given the death sentence."[11]

Camus's subjectivism was checked by his sense of the human condition, and his concern with "identity" by his "essentialism." His gaze is neither local nor "particularist." He may have rejected utopianism and the hubris of grand theory, but he was an acknowledged liberal socialist in the tradition of Jean Jaurès, Léon Blum, and Pierre Mendès-France. His vision is fundamentally humanistic in character. Attempts have been made to appropriate his work for postmodernism or deconstruction.[12] But such attempts necessarily ignore his still-salient perception of the need for reciprocity, his commitment to universal ideals, and his belief in the rule of law. Camus was never a relativist, and a profound belief in the positive or constructive value of reform underpins his critique of all "totalizing action." His attempts to illuminate the human condition, its ab-

---

11. Camus, *Notebooks*, 2: 99.
12. Arthur Kroaker, *The Possessed Individual: Technology and the French Postmodern* (New York, 1992), 6 ff.

surd character, and the need for a constructive response to it also quite obviously take the form of a "grand narrative."

Camus understood the distinction between discursive persuasion and social coercion. He identified with the excluded, but from universalist premises. He was unconcerned with whether any given phenomenon was actually an arbitrary social construct and if he gave expression to the repressed demands of sensual desire, he was not an irrationalist. Quite the contrary: part of the relevance Camus exhibits for the present lies in his attempt to break the equation between freedom and license. His explicit aim was ultimately less a *deconstruction* than a *reconstruction* of freedom. His literature of moral deliberation is a response to the cynicism and relativism of a postmodern age.

Camus was primarily concerned with the *common* existential plight of individuals. But he was always a reluctant activist, and while he demanded positive solutions for pressing social problems, he was basically uninterested in the nuts and bolts of practical politics.[13] There is a romantic streak in Camus. He considered political engagement necessary only in the "extreme situation." But, ironically, it was precisely this extreme situation that his notion of rebellion was designed to prevent.[14] The extreme situation is one in which murder and suicide become relevant issues. They are opposite sides of the same coin: both involve surrendering to the absurd and denying the possibility of

13. "Every time I hear a political speech or I read those of our leaders, I am horrified at having, for years, heard nothing which sounded human. It is always the same words telling the same lies." Camus, *Notebooks*, 1: 18.

14. "One must declare that one is not a revolutionary, but more modestly a reformer. An uncompromising theory of reform. Finally, *and taking everything into consideration,* one may call oneself a rebel." Ibid., 2: 214.

introducing meaning into a meaningless world. The only moral justification for murder, according to Camus, is the willingness to offer one's own life in payment. Whether this actually makes sense in political terms is questionable. Also, for the incurably sick and bedridden, human dignity is perhaps best served by legalizing the right to die. None of this, however, really concerned Camus. His priorities were different. There is a reason he so often employed the mirror as a symbol in his works.

Camus wanted to make people face themselves. He contested the logic by which anonymous masses were murdered by equally anonymous bureaucrats intent on "obeying orders." He never embraced the relativism generated by the human encounter with death and the absence of God. He sought to create a *positive* morality, if not a system of ethics, capable of providing rules for secular conduct. His pessimism was always complemented by an abiding optimism based on a belief in human dignity and the power to learn.

Camus remained a man of the left until the end of his life. In the current conservative context, however, he has been transformed from a critic of the status quo into an avuncular sage. It seems enough to wave a warning finger, chant the word "limit" or "moderation," talk about the eternal themes raised in his work, and caution young people against the radicalism exhibited by the other outstanding, if less sensible, figure of the postwar generation—Jean-Paul Sartre. But this, again, does Camus a disservice. He was no paragon of the anticommunist establishment. He was instead a bohemian and a nonconformist. He was a socialist with syndicalist sympathies, who called on people to make use of civil liberties in deepening democracy, and he tried to develop a new internationalist perspective

on foreign policy. Indeed, from the contemporary perspective, he can be seen as bringing some heart and a new
sense of moral urgency into a socialist democratic movement grown increasingly stale and technocratic.

But Camus's political theory also speaks to the present
in a different way. It boldly, if perhaps unwittingly, breaks
down old distinctions between liberalism, socialism, and
syndicalism. This makes it difficult to categorize him in
terms of one programmatic position. He was a man of the
left, and that was enough. He knew firsthand of the exploitation generated by capitalism and the miseries produced by imperialism. His substitution of rebellion for revolt may have skirted a fact of political life: reform is not
possible under every regime, and revolution can take numerous forms. But his basic insight remains valid: only by
recognizing the vanity of attempting to change everything
is it possible to change some things. This was the sense in
which he envisioned a "creation corrected." It was the title
he imagined for a never-completed final work.

The battle continues: it is still necessary to contest an
unthinking realism in the name of political principle, to
stand *for* something rather than simply against society,
to confront an increasingly complacent conservatism with
a new mixture of liberal socialism. Camus leads us in the
right direction. This makes him a man of our time. But
it also places his thinking politically on the defensive.
And what is true for his politics is equally true for his art.
Camus's popularity, especially among young people, surely
rests on his fiction. But there is a sense in which, ironically,
his *influence* is weakest where it should logically appear
strongest. His attempt to blend classicism with modernism
has fallen by the wayside. His literature of moral deliberation has little in common with the dominant employment

of formalism, postmodern "play," and the calls for uncritical engagement. His themes no longer grip the public in quite the same way as during his lifetime. His humanism is dramatically out of fashion: his cosmopolitanism militates against the provincialism of identity politics; his emphasis on lucidity is challenged by a strident emotionalism; his belief in solidarity is undermined by a new individualism; and his preoccupation with the subtle concerns of religious atheism has seemingly lost its salience. The rebel of the future must contest not only the arrogance of authoritarian political ideologies, but the dominant values of literary production as well.

Camus's work resists the existing state of affairs. Perhaps that is as it should be. Assimilating him, integrating him, means stripping his vision of its power. Camus was a genuinely multicultural thinker whose inspiration derived from two continents, but he never had much use for the jargon of "community." His thinking opposes fashionable forms of ethno-solidarity or ethno-pluralism and his internationalism contests the balkanizing of the globe. Camus was a strong advocate of the United Nations and its World Court, and, by extension, of what would become the European Charter of Social Rights. He may have been guilty of having a "Red Cross mentality," but he had no reason to apologize: such an attitude is necessary for dealing with the human tragedies that lie beyond ideology, for example, the plight of the Vietnamese "boat people" and the genocide in Rwanda. Camus was an apostle of human rights before the term was commonly used, and his belief in solidarity and existential exploration, reciprocity and tolerance, provides a healthy antidote to the conservative verities of the present. His contempt for the whip of the market, his commitment to a liberal socialism, his internationalism, and his suspicion of identity politics speak directly to the political needs of the present.

Camus was neither washed up nor burnt out when he died. His life still lay before him. His experimental spirit, his sense of justice and toleration still emanate from his writings. Camus fought dogmatism with compassion and lucidity, struggled against oppression with bravery and prudence, and served the cause of freedom with dignity and hope. All this makes Camus more than simply the conscience of a bygone age. It makes him the conscience of our own as well.

chronology

1913 Albert Camus is born in Mondovì, Algeria, to Lucien Camus, whose family had settled in Algeria in 1871, and Catherine Sintes, of Spanish origin.

1914 Lucien Camus is killed in the Battle of the Marne during World War I. Catherine Sintes moves into her mother's apartment in the working-class Belcourt neighborhood of Algiers.

1918–23 Attends primary school. Meets Louis Germain.

1924–30 Scholarship student at the Lycées of Algiers. Lives at the home of his uncle, Gustave Acault, and meets Jean Grenier.

1930 Experiences first attack of tuberculosis, and studies are interrupted. Supports himself at various odd jobs.

1931 Creation of the Spanish Republic.

1932   Receives his baccalaureate. Works with Algerian Federation of Young Socialists.

1933   Adolf Hitler takes power in Germany. Camus enters the University of Algiers.

1934   Camus marries Simone Hié. Fascist riots in Paris. Camus joins the Communist Party and is entrusted with propaganda work among the Muslims.

1935   Pierre Laval is invited to Moscow. Disillusionment with the Communist Party begins. Founds the Théâtre du Travail. Works as an actor, director, and playwright.

1936   Electoral victory of the Popular Front. Camus receives his *diplomes d'études supérieures* in philosophy with the thesis *Christian Metaphysics and Neoplatonism.* Travels in central Europe. Marriage to Simone Hié breaks up. Civil war breaks out in Spain. Camus produces his play *The Revolt in Asturia.*

1937   Completes *A Happy Death,* which will remain unpublished during his lifetime. Publication of the essay collection *The Wrong Side and the Right Side.* Supports the Blum-Viollette legislation on mitigating social problems in Algeria. Expulsion from the Communist Party. The Théâtre du Travail turns into the Théâtre de l'Équipe.

1938   End of the Popular Front. Meets Pascal Pia. Camus becomes a journalist for the *Algér-*

Républicain. The Munich Pact is concluded. Camus writes *Caligula.*

1939   World War II begins. Publication of the essay collection *Nuptials.* Camus reports on the Kabylian famine.

1940   Divorce from Simone Hié is finalized. Second marriage to Francine Faure in Lyon. *Algér-Républicain* is banned and Camus loses his job. He leaves Algeria and Pia gets him an editorial position at *Paris Soir.* Camus completes *The Stranger.*

1941   Returns to Algeria. Teaches "French studies" at a private school and completes *The Myth of Sisyphus.*

1942   Publication of *The Stranger.* Returns to the French town of Chambon-sur-Lignon after an outbreak of tuberculosis. Allied landing in North Africa strands him in southern France. Camus will remain separated from his wife until the liberation.

1943   Battle of Stalingrad. Publication of *The Myth of Sisyphus.* Becomes an editor at the publishing house Gallimard, a position Camus will hold until his death. Joins the French Resistance and moves to Paris. Publication of the first *Letter to a German Friend.*

1944   Allied liberation of France. Meets Jean-Paul Sartre, Simone de Beauvoir, Arthur Koestler, Maurice Merleau-Ponty, and Maria Casarès. *The Misunderstanding* is produced. Publication of the next three *Letters to a German Friend*. Becomes editor of the clandestine newspaper *Combat.*

1945 End of World War II. Birth of the Camus twins, Jean and Catherine. *Caligula* is produced. Camus returns to Algeria, where he reports on the brutal repression of anti-imperialist demonstrations in Sétif.

1946 Constitution for the Fourth Republic is ratified. *Neither Victims nor Executioners* is published. Lecture tour of the United States. Controversy with François Mauriac about the punishment of collaborators. Breaks with Merleau-Ponty after a political discussion concerning the Soviet Union.

1947 Publication of *The Plague*. Sartre founds the Rassemblement démocratique et révolutionnaire. Camus condemns the repression of an anti-imperialist revolt in Madagascar.

1948 *State of Siege* is produced. The Iron Curtain falls into place and the cold war begins. Cofounder of Groupe de Liaison Internationale.

1949 Lecture tour of South America. *The Just* is produced. Begins work on *The Rebel.*

1950 New attacks of tuberculosis.

1951 Publication of *The Rebel.*

1952 Controversy with Sartre. Visits Algeria once again. Resigns from UNESCO when Franco's

Spain is admitted to membership. Starts work on the stories for *Exile and the Kingdom* and *The First Man.*

1953 Camus condemns the repression of a workers' revolt in East Berlin. Visits the Sahara.

1954 *Summer* is published. Camus visits Amsterdam. Intervenes for seven Tunisians condemned to death for their political activities. Mendès-France elected premier. Beginning of the Algerian war for independence.

1955 Camus becomes a contributor to *L'Express*. Mendès-France government falls.

1956 Publication of *The Fall*. Produces Faulkner's *Requiem for a Nun*. Soviet repression of the anticommunist uprising in Hungary. Camus appeals for a truce in Algeria. Intervenes in favor of various Algerian liberals and nationalists who have been arrested.

1957 Publication of *Exile and the Kingdom* and "Reflections on the Guillotine." *Caligula* is revived. Camus is awarded the Nobel Prize for literature.

1958 De Gaulle returns to power. The Fifth Republic is established. Camus republishes *The Wrong Side and the Right Side* with a new introduction.

1959 André Malraux, French Minister of Culture, offers Camus artistic control over the Comédie Française, but Camus refuses. He adapts

Dostoyevsky's *The Possessed* and Shakespeare's *Timon of Athens* for the experimental stage. Works full-time on *The First Man*.

1960   Camus is killed in an automobile accident.

1962   Algeria receives independence.

1971   Publication of *A Happy Death.*

1994   Publication of *The First Man.*

index

163

STEPHEN ERIC BRONNER is professor of political science and comparative literature at Rutgers University. He is the author of numerous articles on European politics and culture and the editor of several books. His most important works include *Rosa Luxemburg: A Revolutionary for Our Times, Socialism Unbound, Of Critical Theory and Its Theorists,* and *Moments of Decision: Political History and the Crises of Radicalism,* which was awarded the Michael A. Harrington Prize from the Caucus for a New Political Science.